YOUR
musical
CHILD

Inspiring Kids to Play
and Sing for Keeps

By Jessica Baron Turner, M.A.

EDITOR Jeffrey Pepper Rodgers
PHOTOGRAPHS Gayle Mitchell
Additional Photographs by Danny Edelson

Published by Hal Leonard Corporation
7777 West Bluemound Road
P.O. Box 13819
Milwaukee, WI 53213, USA

Trade Book Division Editorial Offices:
151 West 46th Street, 8th Floor
New York, NY 10036

Visit Hal Leonard online at www.halleonard.com

Printed in the United States of America
First Edition

10 9 8 7 6 5 4 3 2 1

Library of Congress Cataloging-in-Publication Data

Turner, Jessica Baron.
Your musical child : inspiring kids to play and sing for keeps / by Jessica Baron Turner.-- 1st ed.
p. cm.
Includes bibliographical references.
ISBN 1-890490-51-2 (pbk.)
1. Music--Instruction and study--Juvenile. I. Title.
MT1.T93 2004
372.87--dc22
2004000565

Foreword

You may ask yourself why anyone would want to write this book. Why did I? The answers are many, and they all fit together if you take them as a whole. My father loved music and I loved music and, sadly, we had very little ability to share each other's musical passions because we were so different. He was visual/spatial, a whiz at sight-reading who delighted in the subtleties and complexities of classical music. He hoped I'd become another Jacqueline Du Pré as I sawed away on my nemesis, the cello. He would have done anything to help me fall in love with his music. But he didn't have a clue as to where to begin.

Thwarted by my DNA, I was not cut out to follow my father's approach to learning music. An auditory/experiential learner with a visual/spatial deficit, I found the acoustic guitar much more to my liking, along with the oral tradition, poetic lyrics, and folk music. I started wrapping my fingers around the neck of a guitar in second grade, and have been strumming away to my heart's joy ever since. Only out of necessity have I learned to read music in adulthood, and it has taken me hours upon hours of effort to make even the simplest gains. But the labor is paying off in ways I could never have predicted. I only wish it had happened sooner in the hands of the right teacher. I am hoping that this book will help others find the right teachers for their children.

Although my father and I took wonderful walks in one another's musical gardens, we couldn't stay long. If he had understood the nature of my limitations, he might not have felt so critical. Learning styles and learning disabilities are no one's fault. They can be overcome. Had he known how to choose a music instructor who could have unlocked the majesty of classical music for an intuitive thinker, my father and I might have played duets for decades to come.

Only now am I able to begin to comprehend the depth of bliss my father felt listening to Beethoven, Brahms, Schubert, and Haydn. But my father is no longer here to share the wonders of his music, since he passed away in 2002. I often imagine his hands moving with determination over the piano keys, a look of intense concentration flashing across his face. There are other, sweet memories of him listening to a recording of one of his many favorite sonatas, eyes closed, lips smiling as the notes would rise and fall, the tempo staggering as the rondo returned to its theme. I will always see this. I hope this book does his dedication to music justice.

Another concern led me to ask some of the questions about talent and motivation addressed in this book. Many of my friends, identified as a musical prodigies in childhood, look back at their early musical experiences with some frustration or regret. They all tell variations of one story: how pressure to perform and excel eventually stole their joy. Ultimately they burned out and quit performing, and several have stopped playing music entirely. I wondered what might have helped them maintain their positive feelings and creative drive to keep making music over the course of time.

Looking back now, they do not want to blame their parents. They know it's natural for parents to want success for their children. But to maintain a modest and moderate point of view in the presence of young musical genius, parents face some hard decisions. What might they need to know to protect their children's musical futures? I hope I have written a book that encourages both parents and teachers to find a variety of insightful, humanistic ways of working with the very gifted. These and other challenges spurred me on.

I have been fortunate to spend many years in the company of truly inspirational musicians who've made their mark in popular music—folk, pop, rock, reggae, bluegrass, and jazz. All these styles were developed and depend on musicians who learn and think in idiosyncratic ways. Most of my friends learned to play their instruments in nontraditional settings, never following a widely accepted methodology. Few have college degrees, let alone masters degrees in music. Even fewer say they enjoyed traditional school music classes. Each one has broken the mold and crafted a unique style and sound that we, the listening public, enjoy.

Fortunately for these artists and for us, the ability to read and write music and earn a good grade in music class is not a prerequisite for musical artistry, even though such skills help build musical ability and knowledge. Nor does having the ability to read and perform complex music have to inhibit musicians with tremendous originality from inventing music anew. I hope this book encourages parents to appreciate their children's musicality as it emerges in all its diverse forms, and that they will include all styles of music in their definition of what is worth learning. If we can support our children to develop musical competence without narrowing their musical horizons, we will have raised a generation of great new musicians and self-confident adults.

For my father, classical music was the beginning, middle, and end of the journey. The course and boundaries were set for him during childhood. It was not until much later in life that he would allow himself to take forays with me into other musical realms. The results were always surprising and made him feel happy, even expansive for a little while. This late-blooming open-mindedness added breadth and depth to his musical life as it enhanced our mutual understanding. What a gift. Perhaps reading a book like this would have delivered that gift sooner than later.

All of us have untold musical stories, even if they are short ones. I believe we can learn something from sharing these stories; many await you in the pages ahead. So let's talk about what works best in the name of helping our children keep their feet on the sunny side of the street.

I dedicate this book to the memory of two pianists whose passion for music has been inspirational; my great aunt, Sylvia Rosenbloom, and her favorite nephew, my dad, Lewis Raisman Baron.

Acknowledgments

With affection and deepest gratitude, I thank:

David Lusterman, papa of String Letter Publishing, cellist, and progenitor of my writing endeavors, whose personal dedication to abiding musicality inspired, fueled, and shaped the creation of this book.

Jeffrey Pepper Rodgers, whose sensitivity and parental curiosity allowed him to comb through the sandy stretches of this material collecting beach glass while carrying off debris.

To all at Hal Leonard and Adrienne Biggs. Thank you for your infinite creativity, expertise, dedication, drive, and resourcefulness. You are the village that raised this book. I am forever grateful to each one of you.

Carol S. Kelly, Ph.D., my advisor and professor of child development at California State University-Northridge, whose ability to guide students from every walk of life as well as leaders in her field makes this world a better place for our children.

Cecilia Riddell, the inspirational music educator who opened my ears, eyes, hands, and heart to Orff Schulwerk and the work of Zoltán Kodály.

Lois Provda, Ph.D., educational therapist and mentor who generously took me under her wing and shared her knowledge in the realm of learning disabilities.

Dr. Lou Brown, professor of rehabilitation psychology and special education, whose dedication to creating inclusive, mainstreamed education for children with learning differences ignited in me an everlasting dedication to the same purpose.

Vocal coach Seth Riggs, who encouraged my study of the voice, and Andrea Lyons who made learning guitar so fun for a second grader.

The administration, faculty, students, and staff of Westlake Elementary, Bonny Doon Elementary, Natural Bridges Elementary, and Branciforte Elementary in Santa Cruz, California, who have willingly and unwittingly participated in the development of this material for the past three years. Special thanks to Dan Block, David Johnson, Dorothy Franks, and Ken Miller.

Nine brilliant and generous mothers who contributed to the insights, details, logistics, and in some cases, the photographic magic that happens in this book. They include Jennifer Hastings-Porro, Trenise Pot, Debbie Kiva-Smith, Blythe Campbell, Kristina Muten, Christi Bricknell, Lois Graham, Karen Panditi, and Vivian Choy Edelson.

The supportive friends who delicately balance parenting, partnering, and work. Thank you for holding my hand, holding the phone, and helping me take a break every so often. Janis Ost Ford, Nicole Carles, Stephen Mentor, Robin Maxwell, Steve Lawson, Tess Weisbarth, Leslie Baxley, Jennifer Moran Herman, and of course Jen, Trenise, and Debbie.

Gigi and David Addis for your wise counsel and care.

To my precious extended family, Kerry, Rob and Mollyann Davis; Arthur Ost and Janis, Greg, Carina, and Cody Robert Ford; Matt and Sierra Rissman; Lisa, John and Laramie Ruggiero, and to Martin "Godfather" Simpson.

Eric Booth for your passionate and gernerous expertise in arts education. Thank you for lighting my way.

Jessica Lowe Wilson of Music Together and to the folks at Coyote Crossing for giving Gayle Mitchell opportunities to take pictures worth ten thousand words.

All the parents and children who participated in taking photographs for this book. Thank you for your energy, enthusiasm, and generosity.

Those extraordinary musical people I am lucky to count as friends. Thank you for entrusting me with your stories.

Enid Litvak Baron, my mother, who has always sung like a little bird: thank you for sharing your love of folk music and for encouraging and supporting me to become a life-long musician. I'll sing your praises always.

Thanks finally to my partner in life, Rick Turner, and to our precious son, Elias. Without you, this book would never have come to be. Your love, irrepressible creativity, comic interference, patience, timely intelligence, and good-natured help around the house kept me smiling and mostly rational during the years it has taken to write this book. Know that my gratitude and adoration for the two of you runs through every page.

will help you better understand your choices while you seek out the most beneficial resources available. You'll receive information any parent needs to ensure that music becomes and remains a vital part of their children's development. With encouragement, your child will blossom into someone who sings at parties, feels fine about being in school musicals and talent shows, joins the junior high school choir, orchestra, or band, or forms a musical group outside of school. Your child will become a musical participant, someone who continues to play for personal enjoyment throughout life.

If your childhood musical experiences were predominantly positive and fruitful, you are probably addressing your child's musical development very well already. Even so, you may find this book useful, thought provoking, and reassuring. It provides developmental facts and milestones, summaries from current research, and the latest offerings in music instruction and enrichment. The section on learning styles is designed to help you understand your child's particular strengths and challenges as a student (musical and otherwise), and to offer suggestions for tailoring music instruction to fit those learning styles. In the question-and-answer section of this book, you'll hear from a number of parents as they share their stories, examine ideas, and seek new strategies for helping their kids make the most of music.

Since parenting is rarely a straightforward process, I offer this book as a guide and companion for the journey down the long, winding, and beautiful road of your child's musical development.

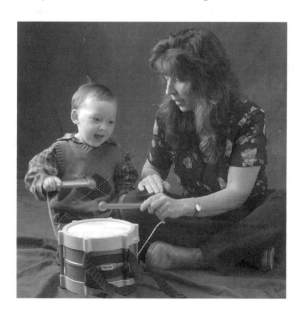

Chapter 1

Parents As Musical Partners

As a parent, whether you have musical training or not, you can nurture your child's musical development by getting and staying involved. Your participation matters a great deal. Children develop their musicality through active endeavors as well as by osmosis. You can take part in both of these processes by seeding their dreams, weeding out the potentially harmful experiences, and helping your children bring their talents to fruition. You can become a role model for your child and a musical companion as well if you take lessons, too, or find ways to make music together. This active participation should make a tremendous difference to your children.

You can *seed* your children's musical dreams by exposing them to music of all kinds. Simply take time to enjoy musical performances together, share recordings and musical literature, and discuss music with your family. How about singing a little? Play the radio in the car. Further along in the book you will find many suggestions for specific musical activities to do with your child. These kinds of experiences will promote children's general knowledge and appreciation of music and raise their musical awareness without requiring them to "work." If you do not already enjoy music daily, you can begin by including musical moments in your routine just a little at a time. Ultimately, these small gains make a big difference.

Simply take time to enjoy musical performances together, share recordings and musical literature, and discuss music with your family.

In the realm of musical study, our children do not need us to be virtuosos. In a sense, the less we know, the more we are able to demonstrate the true value of taking creative risks.

You can *feed* your children's dreams by signing your kids up for music instruction, musical enrichment activities, and by becoming actively involved in the learning process. Some parents choose to take lessons with their children or to study an instrument concurrently. A funny thing happens when both parent and child are music students, learning simultaneously or together. For a brief moment each week, the playing field becomes more level than usual. The power dynamics shift because for one or two shining hours, the parent does not need to shoulder the responsibility of being an expert. At home, you can share the musical adventure, explore together, and reinforce one another's commitment to practice.

In the realm of musical study, our children do not need us to be virtuosos. In a sense, the less we know, the more we are able to demonstrate the true value of taking creative risks. Our kids get to feel better about their own squawks when we squawk right alongside them. We get a bonus prize when we find ourselves laughing together about our honks, flats, and sharps! As we progress together, our sense of accomplishment and our parent-child bond grows and strengthens.

Many successful professional musicians come from families that have played music together at home from the time children were born or soon after. Some of these families have a multigenerational tradition of family music making. It's never too late to start such a tradition, and it takes far less effort than one might imagine. When we casually encourage children to hum into a kazoo or tap on pots and pans for a sing-along with family and friends, our home becomes a kind of comfy classroom.

Taking this relaxed approach provides first-rate nutrition for dreams. Our

kids become familiar with special songs and stories, the voices of fiddle, harmonica, folk harp, or bagpipes. Uncle Bob bellows a Scottish ballad; Aunt Minnie sings a song she learned from her *abuelita* in Mexico; Grandma Rose sings an "aire" or "sher" from the old country; the next-door neighbor belts out an old Broadway favorite, and so on. Musical people who may or may not be formally trained turn into informal teachers and role models without imposing the burden of perfection on a fledgling musician. What a relief, and what fun for everyone.

Along with this kind of informal exposure to music, it's important to help our children develop well-rounded

Signing up for music lessons normally starts with four decisions: when to start, what to study, which methodology or program to choose, and which teacher you believe will best meet the needs of your family.

musical skills. When the time is right, we must introduce our children to formal musical instruction and study. It's best to embark on this journey when we are prepared to pay attention and remain involved with the process. Musical learning, unlike television, does not allow us to click the "on" button and leave the room. Our awareness and concern play essential roles in keeping our children's music lessons positive and productive each week and over time.

If you look around, you'll find so many ways to get started with music—early childhood music classes, movement and music classes, dance classes, group or private music lessons, choir, musical theater workshops, after-school music clubs—all these activities can be pleasurable and productive. Initially sorting through the options can be confusing.

Signing up for music lessons normally starts with four decisions: when to start, what to study, which methodology or program to choose, and which teacher you believe will best meet the needs of your family. Actually, the first decision an informed parent might make is not on this list. The reflective parent asks, "What do I want my child to gain from having a musical experience at this time?" If you can figure that out first, the other decisions will be easier to make. This book was written to help you arrive at trustworthy answers for such questions.

One practical consideration most of us face is the cost of musical study. Setting aside money for music lessons or other after-school extras

Whether or not you feel you are making a financial sacrifice to afford music instruction for your child, it is important to secure your child's commitment beforehand.

presents a real obstacle for so many families. But if you treat music as essential, you will find a way to get your child what he or she needs. Some programs and teachers are less expensive than others; it's always possible to find instruction within your financial reach. You just have to seek it out and ask for what you need.

If cost is an issue for you (as it is for most of us), remember that most group and semi-private lessons cost less than private lessons. Also, many private music teachers allow families in a financial pinch to pay according to a sliding scale. Others help families find scholarship money from local organizations. Paying over time, reducing fees for a short period of time, or taking lessons every other week are just a few ways people work around financial constraints to make music lessons possible.

You might also be able to secure instruction from one of a handful of free or low-cost music programs offered through nonprofit organizations such as the International House of Blues Foundation. These programs are usually locally based, and you can locate them by asking people in your community.

Whether or not you feel you are making a financial sacrifice to afford music instruction for your child, it is important to secure your child's commitment to lessons and practice beforehand. I recommend you spell out for your child what your expectations are, involve him in the decision making, and set reasonable, achievable goals (such as applying himself) for a three-month trial period. After that, you and your child may evaluate the experience and decide whether or not to continue with the original plan or to try something different. If you keep your goals minimal and place an emphasis on what your child has been discovering during the lessons, you will be free to change directions at reasonable intervals, while keeping the entire process positive.

How does a parent choose one particular teacher or program over another? Learning to make music is not a one-size-fits-all procedure, and rules of thumb often seem to have been designed to fit other people's thumbs. Sometimes, people we credit with being experts give mediocre advice. We need a way to sort this out.

Remember that when it comes to your children and how they learn, *you* are the expert. Music instructors know about teaching music. So you have to find a common language with the teacher that lets you work together to ensure the fit and quality of your child's musical instruction. If you do not know much about music, talking about music instruction can feel intimidating. All I can advise here is to ask questions, use

Collaborative decision making with children requires a willingness to listen, negotiate and compromise.

common sense, consider your child, and trust your gut. Let the music teacher meet you halfway by explaining anything that sounds puzzling to you. It's never too late to start learning.

It's good to keep in mind that every teacher has a point of view, personal preferences, and methodological bias that may fit a child at some point in the educational process but may not fit as well at other times. It's up to us to cull the information and choose what our children might relate to and find valuable, then to discuss it and decide whether or not to get started. Along the way, parents continue to monitor the process, making adjustments whenever necessary. We feel and think our way through musical parenting just as we do with everything else.

How much influence *do* you allow your children's feelings and ideas to have on your decision-making process? If you make unilateral decisions and your child resists and fails, you will both lose in the end. If you allow your child to make decisions and he or she chooses unwisely, you'll get poor results, and your child will have cause to doubt himself. This can impact his self-esteem very negatively and cause him to be angry with you for having given him too much freedom to fail.

Collaborative decision making with children requires a willingness to listen, negotiate, and compromise. We want our children to express their ideas and feelings without fear of repercussion, yet we also need them to understand that we are still ultimately in charge. If we strike the right balance, we empower our children to actively shape their futures without burdening them with too much responsibility for making honest mistakes. (That comes in time no matter what we do.)

If you are a "my way or the highway" style parent, this is going to present a challenge. If you say "Piano!" and she says "Drums!" you may wind up with no lessons at all. Engaging your child in an open

Choosing to give yourself time to make informed decisions could be the most critical decision of all.

discussion might be something new for you. If you remember a time when you pushed too hard and your child pushed back, maybe you'll consider doing things a little differently. Many of us avoid negotiating with our children out of fear that we might be persuaded to give in and live to regret it. But if we approach musical learning as an adventure, on an open-ended ticket, we can avoid power struggles completely. We can become our children's partners on the journey.

Certain experiences tend to polarize adults and children. Choosing which instrument to play is one that deserves some serious time and consideration. Many parents feel stumped when it comes to this important early decision. The choices can cause confusion or bring on some additional external pressure. When the band director recommends trombone and you know your child tires easily, likes quiet, and prefers the flute, should you ask about flute instead? Maybe the string teacher says, "We need a cellist for the school orchestra," your spouse says, "she'd be great on bassoon." But you know your child weighs 50 pounds and stands 49 inches and likes violin. What should you do? The wrong decision is any decision that excludes your child, and the right decision may carry with it other unpleasant consequences. Hopefully the section ahead on selecting a musical instrument will prove helpful to you.

At each step of your child's musical journey, *your* patience, curiosity, and determination will serve him well. Choosing to give yourself time to make informed decisions could be the most critical decision of all. A carefully planned first experience should lead to a second. A bad first experience may eliminate any chance of a second. Along the way, our children can benefit from our active involvement.

For example, one area in which every child needs a supportive partnership with their parent is performing. Performance skills do not come naturally to most children. Only one or two in any class are what parents lovingly refer to as "a ham." Yet many young music students are expected to perform, sometimes right off the bat or within the first year of study.

This emphasis on musical learning as a product detracts from its value as a creative process when children are prematurely pressured to present what they've accomplished. Performances can be valuable experiences for kids but only when they are really ready to share. But the

financial stability of many public arts education programs depends on getting donations
from members of the community who attend
recitals and concerts. Once people donate,
they want to hear what and whom they've
funded! So out come the kids, onstage, ready
or not.

As your child's partner, you can help his
teacher decide when and how to include him
in a recital or performance. Making music is
by nature a highly personal experience. We
are drawn to make music partly because it
gives us a personal sense of satisfaction, creativity, and wonder. But young beginners
often feel embarrassed by their poor tone

The primary goal of the developmental framework is to build our understanding of children's musical potential without turning milestones into measuring sticks.

and lack of grace. In light of the greatness of the music, new players are
prone to shrink at the notion of playing in front of other people. It takes
a very special music teacher to teach performance skills in a manner that
serves children well.

Children also need our partnership in evaluating and celebrating
their progress. They can usually tell when their playing is getting better,
but they want to hear it from us. If we are not musically inclined, how
do we know they are improving? We need some criteria on which we
can base our observations, and we must have a sense of what to expect
from our young music students over time. The developmental framework in the next chapter of this book is designed to respond to this need
in a general way, laying out children's musical development one year at
a time. Of course there is no "average"child, so a framework presents a
picture of progress that applies a little to everyone yet to no one child
completely. The primary goal of the developmental framework is to
build our understanding of children's musical potential without turning
milestones into measuring sticks.

Developmental descriptions may prove helpful because our child's
musical development is complex and idiosyncratic. Many specific and
interrelated skills are coming along at the same time. We want to know
what to look for rather than waiting to hear from the teacher about our
child's progress. Please use the framework to empower yourself so you
can notice what your child is doing and feeling.

Each week, our children should be making small improvements in one or two skill areas. But these changes may be small, subtle, and hard to notice. They might even be conceptual. An improved bowing arm, a slightly more curved wrist, recognition of a new note on the paper: each skill is critical. Eventually, all the little skills start sounding like bigger ones—that's when a child's playing comes together in a noticeable way. At such times, it's easy to mark the improvements and deliver some heartfelt praise. Yet our children have been laboring away for weeks making tiny gains that we could have been taking into account all along if we had only known what to look for. That's where the framework comes in; it helps us gaze into the distance to catch a glimpse of the big picture. It allows us to ask our child's teacher more specific questions about what our child is learning.

Being our child's musical partner involves some cooperative navigation across the terrain of time and opportunity. The course of musical study can prove somewhat unpredictable and inconsistent. Months of motivated lessons, months of no lessons; burning interest in one thing eclipsed by something else; an urgent plea to join the school band and play Sousa, followed by blaring rock music on the boom box at home. But compared to the predictable stretch of road children have traditionally traveled while learning to play classical music, the scenic and uncharted route can prove more enjoyable over the long haul. We all know that taking a cross-country drive without a map is probably foolhardy, but in the moments that we most fear we are lost, we begin to notice things we'd have otherwise missed. It can be fun to get lost, as long as we have a compass.

With music, too, the broad-minded and well-informed parent expects things to go differently than planned, and understands that these moments are an unexpected invitation to adventure. Simply put, the course of a child's music education is like everything else in life; change is inevitable and change can be good. Even quitting, when it's a symptom of needing to change teachers or approaches, can be good. Children change, their personalities expand, their skills develop, their priorities shift. The course of their music education reflects those changes. Yet our first response when we hear that our kids want to quit lessons or stop playing an instrument is

Simply put, the course of a child's music education is like everything else in life; change is inevitable and change can be good.

usually disappointment or panic. Some of us remember that when we quit long ago; perhaps we quit forever.

Now we may feel that this was a mistake. We may say we wish they had made us practice, but we remember how much we wished at the time that they wouldn't force the issue.

The Braid Model strives to be developmental, pragmatic, and realistic.

There should have been another way to handle the situation, but most people had no idea what that might have been. How could they? Musical success was defined in narrow terms, and outside of being a prodigy, there was only one way to achieve it.

We want things to be different for our children. Fortunately, the world has evolved and changes are not only possible, they are necessary. This is what motivated me to develop a new model for musical development: the Braid Model. It takes a flexible, multifaceted approach to helping our children become active, creative musical people in today's busy world. The Braid Model strives to be developmental, pragmatic, and realistic. It gives children room to be kids and parents room to figure things out as they go. It asks music teachers and parents to become musical partners in children's musical growth and development. It gives every child, every learner, a chance to be successful. Here's how it works.

Imagine children's musical development as a braid with three stands. One strand of this musical braid represents what children soak up through daily exposure to music in the world. This *experiential strand* contains music at school and entertainment in the home, on the car radio, at a friend's house, at the arcade, at the theater, on the playground. Children experience music almost everywhere they go. Many of them hum, sing with friends, mimic commercials. They listen, they hear, they create.

Another strand contains what children learn from music teachers and through other forms of musical instruction. This is the *instructional strand*.

Finally, the *self-discovery strand* is what children discover and gain on their own. When they get inspired to make music independently, their own creativity leads the way. This happens alone, with friends, and with us. We can nurture development in the third strand by participating in activities that encourage musical experimentation.

When we make a braid, we drop one strand to pick up a different one. The braid itself embraces the dropped strand, holding it in place just where we left it until we can pick it up once more. The braid continues growing as we cross the strands one over another. We drop the one we previously held and pick up the one we released before. All three strands keep coming in and out of the braid until it is complete.

Just so with musical development. Some months, our children study hard and spend a lot of time acquiring new skills in music lessons (the instructional strand). Concurrently, they may also benefit from experimenting with their own ideas and sharing their experiences with us through conversation and demonstration (the self-discovery strand). During these times, if you have less time to spend going to musical events or playing recordings together, your child will still be making steady musical progress.

Some months, our children stop lessons, but they play around with music on their own (the self-discovery strand). At such times, they'll tend to integrate what they've learned in lessons, finding new ways to please themselves with what they know. They might make music in a school music class, play in an ensemble, or join a garage band, but if you ask them if they want to take music lessons again, they're likely to say no. Even so, their musical understanding will be deepening as they reach new levels of mastery. Some people refer to this as "woodshedding."

At times like these, a parent can pick up the experiential strand and get tickets to a concert, share a musical biography out loud after dinner, or rent a musical film for the family to watch together. This can also be a good time for Mom or Dad to start music lessons!

When parents study music formally, it weaves the instructional strand into family life in a brand new way. Someone at home is practicing, even if Junior is not. And if Mom or Dad are playing an instrument, Junior may find it nearly impossible to resist asking for a turn. (He may also ask to start music lessons again, but don't count on that.)

Using the Braid Model, we can expect that at various points in time, we are going to let go of the instructional strand for a while. Sometimes kids need to take a short break from formally studying music and the instructional strand. Under extreme circumstances, even the self-discovery strand may be left dangling for a bit while we work with the experiential strand. Nevertheless, the other two strands stay in place, held fast by past achievements.

A child may want time just to practice and play around with techniques and ideas he already knows. He might need a quiet space and a couple hours of undisturbed time to noodle around with his instrument.

Or he may need to pay more attention to other activities, giving less time to music than usual.

Almost every child spends time on other interests—sports or drama activities, clubs, or summer camp. These activities make a well-rounded person. You find yourself wondering whether allowing your child to take a break from lessons is going to be the beginning of the end. But your child can still be musically active during "experiential" months, listening to music, going to musical plays, movies, or concerts, or even reading about music in novels and the news.

Almost every child spends time on other interests— sports or drama activities, clubs or camp. These activities make a well-rounded person.

During these times, you can do some things to make sure your child continues to enjoy making music, too. Playing music together informally at home, or asking him to play something for you or to help you with a musical project for a holiday or family occasion could help keep the self-discovery strand in play. Your role facilitating musical activities once in a while could become an essential ingredient in keeping your child's musical development going. Braiding the self-discovery strand with the experiential strand can bring enough rich music through your child's life to reawaken his or her desire to study.

Over time, the musical braid grows with the inclusion of all three strands. Keeping them in sight or in play guarantees that your child will receive enough stimulation, instruction, support, and reinforcement to pursue his or her musical potential and dreams. When you or your child feel the need to release a strand for a while, simply pick up another one in its place. When you can, remember to pick up the old strand again. It's best to do that before or during the next summer or school year if at all possible. Continuing to bring all three strands through the musical braid in a timely manner will result in strong and steady growth.

This Braid Model is partly informed by D. W. Winnicott's concept of "good-enough mothering," a well-known theory in the fields of child development and psychology. It lays the foundation for the notion that, given enough love, security, and understanding, children can learn to tolerate a certain amount of frustration, benign neglect, and parental fumbling. Pain and loss are natural parts of life, so all children benefit in the long run from acquiring good coping skills. It follows that, in

As parents, what we ultimately fail to provide will become theirs to seek.

light of these truths, perfect parenting would be tragic; it would prevent our children from becoming creative, resilient, and resourceful. But they also need to know they are secure in their familial relationships in order to make the best use of those less-than-idyllic experiences.

So we might consider the Braid Model as a very distant cousin of good-enough mothering (parenting). It tells us that, as parents, we can hope to provide a good portion of what our children need in order to develop musically. What we ultimately fail to provide will become theirs to seek. This sets us free from the start because we assume that we will not be able to do it all. We can grant ourselves permission to relax a little and do whatever we can. We all need the freedom to make adjustments and shift priorities without feeling panicked or wrong. We need some "wiggle room" when it comes to prioritizing and scheduling our children's activities. The braid lets us have all that. We can change directions, approaches, teachers, classes, or instruments when we deem it to be in our children's best interest. As long as we keep two strands in hand and the third in view, our children will be making excellent musical progress.

SEVENTEEN RULES
OF THE MUSICAL ROAD

1. Stand firm in your commitment to your child's music education. Your child will benefit from hearing a clear message that making music is important and valuable.

2. If you want to raise a musical child, be a musical adult. Do it any way you can. Take lessons of your own, join a choir, watch music instruction videos, just get going. You will set a great example and give your child a musical partner at home.

3. Find kind, thoughtful, experienced teachers for your child. Ask for their references so you can talk to current or former pupils. Look before you leap.

4. Participate in your child's music lessons when appropriate. Coming into lessons for the first and last five minutes helps your child get settled and keeps you current with what she is learning.

5. Strive for excellence but don't push for perfection.

6. Motivate and inspire your child to engage fully in making music rather than pressuring him to succeed.

7. Show your child how to turn mistakes into opportunities for learning. Focusing on the artistic process instead of worrying about achieving goals makes learning fun.

8. Every once in a while, appear to pay no attention whatsoever to your child's musical doings so she can create in privacy. Then spy.

9. When your child expresses negative feelings about music lessons, take a closer look at the situation. Ask for specific feedback. Try to put your child's reactions in perspective. Feel entitled to observe the lessons in action. Then, if the facts suggest that a change is in order, make one. Do not wait around hoping things will "get better."

10. When it comes to enforcing a practice schedule, be flexible. Occasionally hand out a "Get Out of Jail Free" card. But whatever you do, keep listening.

11. If practicing becomes problematic for your child, find ways to adjust her approach. Do not let practice problems escalate. Change is good.

12. When rendering praise, be sincere, specific, generous, and discreet.

13. If you'd like your child to play for friends and family, extend a gentle invitation. If she accepts, wonderful. If not, perhaps she'll choose to share her talents with others in the future. Refrain from offering a bribe!

14. Keep a record or a journal marking your child's musical experiences and high points. Include art, photos, and creative writing. This will make his efforts easy to see and celebrate.

15. Enjoy music together every chance you get.

16. As a medium, music's rich possibilities extend beyond the reaches of our imaginings. Its power to touch our hearts and communicate what words can barely contain is truly mysterious. Share the mystery with your child. Allow curiosity to be your guide. Keep asking questions.

17. Try to contain your public bragging to times you're sure your little prodigy is out of earshot. For some children, getting too much attention can be almost as embarrassing as getting none at all. But do remember to brag at least a little just to see him roll his eyes and give you a goofy smile.

Chapter 2

Ages and Stages of Musical Development

Since the 1970s, learning theorists and educators have been touting the concept of the whole child. In simple terms, this means addressing all the ways a child learns and functions instead of trying to help her learn just one thing, just one way. This not only increases the odds she'll "get the lesson," it means she'll enjoy learning and find ways to apply what she has learned. For instance, addition is not just a math skill to be done with a pencil and paper. You can teach a child to add through games, music, movement, problem solving, science, nature, art, and cooking. Then she will understand addition and know its relevance, and she will instinctively apply addition skills to activities such as arts and crafts, drawing, dance, and music.

Where musical development is concerned, the whole-child concept fits. We hear, see, move large and small muscles, sequence, remember, understand, interpret, time, cooperate, communicate, imagine, take creative risks, express, and feel. When we make music, we are using many different but integral parts of ourselves.

Even a brief musical act, such as reading and bowing a single note on the violin, requires that your child coordinate several skills and sensitivities.

By noticing and addressing the details of how our children approach and perform this confluence of tasks, we parents are better able to gauge their abilities and needs as developing musicians. We can pay attention to the things they do well. We can note what they find challenging. We can consider, together with the music teacher, how these various parts interact and affect each other. This will help us understand our children as whole people and whole musicians.

In fact, even a brief musical act, such as reading and bowing a single note on the violin, requires that your child coordinate several skills and sensitivities at one time. Through her visual system and memory, she reads the note on the piece of sheet music. She interprets this note's value and pitch. Remembering and hearing pitches accurately from experience, she decides where to place her finger along the fingerboard of her violin to create that specific note. Simultaneously, her memory tells her how hard to press down on the string with her finger. Across her chest, her upper body strength and muscle memory in her neck and bowing arm determine the angle, amount of power, and the speed at which she pulls the bow across the strings to create good tone for that note. She is also calculating the amount of bow to bring across the strings to make that note last for the correct amount of time. She does all these jobs in a split second—all to play that single note. What a breathtaking feat.

With this in mind, it's easy to understand how when one kind of sensing or one skill area is inefficient, underdeveloped, or in any way disabled, your child's musicianship can be affected. To gain a clearer understanding of your child's strengths and challenges, observe her musical activity carefully and talk with her teacher about anything you've noticed. Ask detailed questions. Together, you may increase one another's understanding to help your daughter realize her greatest potential.

It's easy to understand how when one kind of sensing or one skill area is inefficient, underdeveloped, or in any way disabled, your child's musicianship can be affected.

Before we look at the developmental framework that follows, let's face the facts about what we do to ourselves and our kids when we make comparisons. Most of us, at some time in our childhood, get the notion that other people know more than we do. As true as it may be, this realization can make us feel pretty inadequate. Most of us come to accept our shortcomings, but when we read developmental information, the self-critical little voice in our heads can still make us feel edgy and vulnerable. We may question whether or not our kids are smart enough, disciplined enough, creative enough. We worry we may have fallen short somehow in our parenting. What a grind! As the designer of these charts, I implore you not to take the information too seriously. It's accurate and based on research and experience, but by no means must all children awaken to their musical potential at these specific ages and stages.

If we view our children's musical development in terms of absolute developmental norms, more than 50 percent will fall either behind or ahead of the curve.

If we view our children's musical development in terms of absolute developmental norms, more than 50 percent will fall either behind or ahead of the curve. Yet every child is special and wonderful and capable of becoming a musical person at his or her own pace. Your knowledge of your own child has more validity than anything you'll read here or anywhere else. No need to fret if your child's musical development falls outside the norms. Do not be surprised to discover that your child has not yet accomplished tasks achieved by other children his age. Late bloomers are a large enough group to merit their own cliché. Better late than never.

Conversely, do not be too surprised to find your child accomplishing tasks in the framework much earlier than average. Your child might be musically brilliant. He may simply have peaked before the pack, and his abilities will level out at some point. In either case, making music will be fun and rewarding for him, and you can feel good about his progress.

Your child's grasp and mastery of musical skills will result from a combination of physical maturity, genetic coding, emotional readiness, life experience, exploration, and instruction—both formal and informal. When all these elements line up just right, a child accomplishes something remarkable. You can play a significant part in helping that process along by taking the following developmental descriptions into consideration and in stride.

Birth to One Year

HEARING

♪ **Newborn (birth to four months):** A newborn usually reacts suddenly to loud sounds through movements such as widening the eyes, jumping, or extending the arms and legs. Parents should look for signs of localization from their child. Localization is eye movement or turning the head toward the direction of the sound source.

♪ **Three to six months:** Babies at this age should turn and search out a different sound. They should also be able to respond to the sound of their name. During this particular developmental time, the baby will play with sounds by cooing and babbling. The baby should smile or stop crying when either of the parents speaks to him/her. In addition, the baby should act differently to the ways the parents talk to him/her (angry, friendly, loving).

♪ **Six to ten months:** A baby at this age should be able to seek out the sound source. When his or her name is called, the baby should look toward the speaker. In addition, the baby should respond to both soft and loud sounds. Familiar sounds such as a doorbell ringing or a dog barking should get a response from the baby. The baby should also pay attention when the parents talk to him/her.

♪ **Ten to 12 months:** A baby will begin to increase his or her babbling, which will more closely resemble speech. The baby plays with sounds and is able to put sounds together in different patterns.

These descriptions come from the Academy of Pediatrics.

MUSICAL AWARENESS

♪ Infants notice and respond to sounds and musical tones in their environments.

♪ Infants like to explore many sources of sound to see what they'll do. This natural curiosity can help them discover ways to begin making music by themselves.

♪ They are indiscriminately receptive to every kind of linguistic sound they hear until they reach six months of age, at which time they begin to focus only on the sounds they hear most often.

♪ Infants are soothed by calm parental singing, and are stimulated by exciting, rhythmic music.

PITCH DEVELOPMENT

♪ At 12 months of age, infants' brains become less receptive to sounds they do not hear frequently. Exposing infants to pitched music before this stage helps them integrate music as a normal, perhaps even dominant, experience.

♪ Infants learn to make vocal sounds that correlate to pitches as they develop language. This is the beginning of vocal inflection, the rising and falling of our speaking voices. Parents can help this process along by talking and vocally playing with their infants. This includes responding to babies' babbling by echoing and repeating what the babies say. This form of interaction can be very musical if the conversation includes snippets of melody and song. Studies show that infants have the capacity to perceive and mentally organize music. They detect slight differences in pitches played in order. They even react to single note changes in familiar melodies!

RHYTHMIC DEVELOPMENT AND MOVEMENT

♪ Infants perform and experience their first natural large-motor body rhythms when they raise and lower their arms together in brief repeating patterns, play pat-a-cake, crawl, and then, as toddlers, walk. Until now, they've heard rhythms in their environment and felt rhythms while moving and being rocked or bounced. Now they can start to create rhythms independently.

♪ They enjoy playing rhythmic musical games that include movement such as "This Little Piggy" and "The Noble Duke of York." The unbeatable blend of rhythmic movement, language development, song, and affection boosts their basic musicality.

♪ Parents who play recorded music for their infants while reinforcing the steady beat or pulse with gentle physical contact such as clapping, bouncing, tapping, dancing together, and rocking can help them develop a sense of rhythm.

INSTRUMENTAL DEVELOPMENT

♪ Infants like to hear percussive sounds made with toys and small hand-held percussion instruments. If shown how to shake a rattle or hit a drum, they are likely to imitate the musical behavior, master the motion, and then play the instrument for several seconds, independently, while being held or supported physically by a caregiver.

♪ Many infants respond happily to the sound of an acoustic guitar or other stringed instrument being strummed nearby while they lie on their backs and kick or wave their arms. Once they crawl, they will gravitate to the guitar, slap it, or pull on the strings.

♪ Infants often enjoy sitting on their caregiver's lap at the piano and listening to her press down on one key at a time. Many infants will attempt to copy this motion to make the sound. The single note playing will be followed by one hand or two banging on the keys to great effect.

♪ Infants respond to the range of pitches on the piano, most often preferring the high notes to the lower ones. This may also be true of other instruments although current research addressing this point does not exist at this time.

COGNITIVE DEVELOPMENT

♪ Studies show that infants who participate in frequent sing-song exchanges with caregivers demonstrate greater levels of linguistic and academic achievement later in life. Studies also show that these children become better problem solvers. It's possible that the range of vocal inflections they hear and interpret, and to which they respond, may help them think creatively from a very young age.

Rhythmic Musical Activities for Infants

♪ Here are a few fun suggestions for ways to keep time to music with very young children:

- While she sits in your lap, tap the backs of her shoulders to the beat with your fingertips.

- While she sits in your lap, clap her hands inside of yours to the beat.

- Hold her hands and raise her arms a little and then lower them in time to the beat.

- While she lies down on her back, hold her feet and move her legs in a bicycling motion. (This is also great for children's digestion.)

- While she lies down on her back, open her arms, then bring her hands back together over her tummy to the beat of the music, in an "open them/shut them" game.

- Bounce her gently on your knees.

- Sway with her from side to side, her feet perched on yours.

- Tap her knees and shoulders to the beat with your fingertips. Invite her to tap your knees and shoulders, too.

- Play hand-clapping games, such as pat-a-cake, to different pieces of music.

One to Two Years

HEARING

♪ **12 to 15 months:** A toddler begins to increase his or her babbling, which more closely resembles speech. The toddler plays with sounds and is able to put sounds together in different patterns.

♪ **15 to 18 months:** A toddler is able to directly localize to most sounds. In addition, the child can understand simple phrases, identify familiar objects such as body parts, and follow simple directions. A child at 18 months should have an expressive vocabulary of 20 or more words and short phrases.

MUSICAL AWARENESS

♪ Instrumental music and especially songs that feature dramatic musical changes—high and low, fast and slow, stop (rests) and go (notes)—foster in toddlers the awareness of musical dynamics.

♪ Toddlers recognize favorite music and show excitement when they know a song.

♪ Toddlers respond to the various moods of music even though they are too young to understand their own reactions. Scary music causes them to feel fearful. Jolly music winds them up for play. Soft music relaxes them at the right time and can annoy them if they're ready for action instead.

PITCH DEVELOPMENT

♪ Toddlers can explore pitch with a variety of instruments (see Instrumental Development).

♪ Toddlers develop a more heightened sense of pitch by listening to songs and humming or singing those songs with adults.

♪ Toddlers do not usually sing in tune, although a few can. Repeating a song that always starts and ends on the same note is a good way to help them establish a sense of "home pitch."

♪ Toddlers who are able to speak usually begin to participate in singing with single words or brief responses. They learn fragments of melodies (for example, the words *twinkle, twinkle* in "Twinkle, Twinkle Little Star"). Sometimes they sing the fragments in the right context within a song, but more often than not, they sing randomly and repeat the same fragments.

♪ Toddlers like to play musical games with caregivers. Musical finger-play songs that include repeated lines such as "Where Is Thumbkin?" and songs with line repetition such as "Frère Jacques" allow toddlers to hear a line and then copy it, if they are able.

♪ Toddlers experiment with pitch register and vocal inflections as they begin to use language to express their feelings and ideas in songs, both learned and of their own creation. This important foray into creative self-expression often results in little musical treasures that merit tape recording at home and letters to relatives!

RHYTHMIC DEVELOPMENT AND MOVEMENT

♪ Toddlers are able to feel and move to a steady beat naturally when they perform large motor movements such as crawling and walking. They move rhythmically all day long: clapping, crawling, walking, running, rolling, swinging arms, jumping, shaking various parts of the body.

♪ Toddlers acquire their first natural sense of tempo when they gain control over the pace at which they move. Play music at different tempos (or speeds) for your child and dance or move together. You may notice his movements adapt to each selection.

♪ A toddler's intrinsic sense of rhythm is inconsistent. Sometimes you can hear a steady beat when she shakes a rattle or pounds a drum. Sometimes her rhythm wanders or drifts away. This is a good stage to play copying and echoing games with percussion instruments or homemade instruments such as pots and pans. Play a short rhythmic phrase and ask your toddler to play it back. Then copy her next phrase, whatever that might be. If you keep an open mind and require no accuracy, you can engage her at deeper and deeper levels of musical play.

PITCH DEVELOPMENT

♪ The ability to hear and distinguish between one pitch and another is developing quickly in preschool children.

♪ Preschoolers may be able to sing the central or home pitch of a song (*do*) in relatively good tune, and they might also be able to sing the dominant note above (*sol*) in tune as well. Some children struggle with these pitches at this age, while others find them easy to hear and sing.

♪ Most preschool children are able to recognize the difference between high and low tones once they've been taught what to listen for.

♪ With some music education, preschoolers begin to distinguish whether notes performed in a sequence are getting higher or lower, in other words whether a scale is ascending or descending.

RHYTHMIC DEVELOPMENT AND MOVEMENT

♪ Preschoolers happily link songs and music with movement. Walking, rocking, dancing, and clapping are just a few kinds of movements that give kids a chance to feel rhythms with their entire bodies. They begin to associate melodic passages with certain kinds of steps and moves. And when it's time to remember how the music goes, moving around can bring it all back. So finger-play and movement songs are very engaging for children at this stage.

♪ Unpitched percussion instruments suit most children in this age group, as well as pitched Orff instruments with removable bars such as glockenspiels, xylophones, and marimbas. The Orff instruments provide preschoolers with a means to explore melodic music making without the acquisition of fine motor skills or the ability to read music.

♪ They can begin to copy rhythm patterns in short sequences, combining long and short beats in a variety of interesting ways. As they learn to count, they can often count beats in numbers of two, three, or four, the numbers of beats we most often hear in Western music. Parents who engage in rhythmic pattern play combining, for example, a long beat followed by two short beats (tom-tom rhythm) can encourage their children to copy the pattern, then add something new to it. Building rhythmic patterns and phrases, especially on fun instruments, makes for a great musical adventure.

♪ Beat sequences longer than four can be challenging for preschool children to play, but they need to hear longer sequences if they are going to internalize those meters. It's great to move with them to music in less common time signatures such as in African or Indian music. Their minds grasp more musical possibilities this way.

INSTRUMENTAL DEVELOPMENT

♪ The singing voices of preschoolers are naturally high because their vocal chords are short. They rarely sing below a G note in the octave beneath middle C.

♪ Some four-year-olds are able to participate appropriately in group instrumental lessons. The same "kindergarten readiness skills" they may be working on at preschool (such as sitting still, listening, following directions, taking turns, raising their hands) get a good workout in a music class. These classes usually serve as an introduction to making music rather than requiring children to work hard at accomplishing musical tasks.

♪ Some musically motivated three- and four-year-olds can strum ukuleles and small guitars or play simple melodic keyed instruments as well as percussion. Suzuki recommends beginning children in violin lessons at this age, although in some cases they do not actually play the instrument until they're able to stand, hold, and bow a makeshift violin-like box instrument.

♪ Preschoolers whose melodic awareness is blossoming on the early side may express a desire to learn to play a melodic instrument. The question then is whether or not they are ready to handle such an instrument. Parents interested in starting their young children with instrumental study this early in life may find ways to adapt the instrument or expectations to the child's ability to play or learn.

♪ Few preschool-age children are psychologically ready to practice an instrument. Formal private musical training only rarely begins this early in life. (Musical prodigies are sometimes an exception to the rule.)

♪ Three- and four-year-olds who are enrolled in group music lessons typically enjoy and benefit from singing and dancing during class, as well learning to play an instrument.

SINGING AND LEARNING SONGS

♪ Preschoolers learn to sing songs by repeating them, one or two lines at a time, until they've memorized an entire song or a portion of it. This call-and-response technique makes use of their new abilities to sing through imitation.

♪ Preschoolers usually remember a few lines of a song they've sung many times. For this reason short songs (one verse only) are usually favored. Add-on songs in which the verse is always the same except for one element, such as a species of animal or the part of a machine or bus, are also big hits with the three- and four-year-old set.

COMPOSITION

♪ When preschoolers experiment with notes and melodies, the melodic contour of their musical creations often sounds random and funny. Their fledgling compositions might feature a single line from a song they are learning at the time, and the most obvious difference between one note and another is often register (high, low, or monotonous). The most prevalent dynamic features in preschool music making are volume (very soft or too loud) and tempo (calm or warp speed).

♪ When preschoolers make melodies, they are almost always linked with language. A preschooler might explore a fun word such as *elephant* by singing it many times, shifting his voice, or stretching and shrinking syllables like auditory Silly Putty and Shrinky Dinks (remember those?). The words and music are inseparable because these children are acquiring skills in both music and language at the same time.

♪ Preschoolers can be subtle and indirect communicators. From time to time, their personal songs candidly reveal their moods, topics of interest, and questions that occupy their young minds. You can sometimes gain a window into your preschooler's inner sanctuary by listening without comment to those tiny songs as they tumble out during a long ride in the car or soak in the tub. At such times we are prone to wonder why we don't have the tape recorder handy!

COGNITIVE DEVELOPMENT

♪ Intellectually speaking, preschool children experience music as pure sound. They do not analyze what they hear or attempt to reorganize it. Typically, higher order thinking does not play a significant role in how young children experience music until around six years of age. For this reason, exposure to singing and music of all kinds helps preschool-age children acquire musical skills naturally and effortlessly.

♪ The same part of our brains processes both language and music. Studies show a correlation between early exposure to music and the development of outstanding verbal, linguistic, and verbal problem-solving abilities later in childhood. Verbal preschoolers may also be musically active preschoolers, although the reverse is not always the case!

♪ Preschoolers are beginning to gain a very basic awareness of numbers. Parents can play rhythm games that double as early math exercises, inviting children to count, sequence, and play or move to two different kinds of beats (fast, slow, short, long).

Five to Six Years

MUSICAL AWARENESS

♪ Five- and six-year-olds are learning to conserve melodies, meaning they can remember them and recognize them even when the key, tempo, or underlying rhythms are changed. Nevertheless, they still depend on hearing lyrics when they try to identify the titles of the melodies.

♪ They love playing around with musical dynamics: changing tempos, volume, moods, and tones. They can infuse music with imaginative play, pretending to perform it in character, for instance, as a beloved cartoon or fairy-tale personality. A good game of conductor is fun for them; they direct everyone else to sing at a particular tempo, then speed it up and slow it down as they please.

PITCH DEVELOPMENT

♪ Kindergartners and first-graders are beginning to be able to accurately sing the home note or *do* of any song, familiar or new. Music instruction that includes ear training at this age helps solidify their ability.

♪ Five- and six-year-olds should be able to accurately match their voices to the pitches *do*, *mi*, and *sol*. Many can sing songs relatively in tune if they started making and appreciating music at an earlier stage.

RHYTHMIC DEVELOPMENT AND MOVEMENT

♪ Since kindergarten and first-grade children like to play rhythmic patterns with percussion instruments, they begin to show an interest in stringing their own rhythm patterns together.

♪ Five- and six-year-olds are capable of connecting two different durations of notes in rhythm patterns. They can learn to call short and long notes by rhythmic syllables (such as *ti* or *ta*) or by their formal names (such as quarter and half notes).

♪ They like to express rhythms using their whole bodies; large motor activities with arms, legs, feet, hands, heads, and hips (think "Hokey-Pokey") and fine motor activities such as blinking both eyes or wiggling one finger can become rhythmically expressive activities. At this age, movement and rhythm go hand in hand.

INSTRUMENTAL DEVELOPMENT

♪ Most five- and six-year-olds have developed enough coordination, self-control, and focus to participate in instrumental music lessons.

♪ The developmental window for learning to make music is wide open at this age. If they form a good relationship with the teacher, and if the activities presented during lessons are engaging, children can develop what will eventually seem like a "natural" ability to play an instrument.

♪ Many kindergartners and first-graders do not wish to practice an instrument every day unless the experience is brief and playful. Handling the issue of practice thoughtfully will prove key to your young child's motivation to study an instrument.

MUSIC THEORY

♪ Kindergartners and first-graders are old enough to begin learning to read music through interactive games and activities. With proper, developmentally appropriate instruction, they can read eighth and quarter notes and vocalize the notes using rhythmic syllables such as *ti* and *ta* to show their duration and placement in a rhythmic sequence.

♪ Kindergartners and first-graders can begin to read melodic notation by studying the placement of notes on the musical staff, particularly if they start reading just two notes, such as *do* and *sol* (C and G). Learning simple theory can be as simple as learning the alphabet if the music teacher makes the experience playful and uses materials that make information and ideas easy to remember.

♪ Children at this age are ready to learn to count and play rhythms in meters of three and four beats; they can begin to learn to notate these patterns using conventional or "artistic" representational notation.

♪ Six-year-olds can play extremely simple contrapuntal rhythms in an ensemble, given appropriate leadership. For instance, one group can play a steady beat while another plays a skipping rhythm at the same time. They can appreciate the syncopation and find such rhythm jams fun and exciting.

SINGING AND LEARNING SONGS

♪ Five- and six-year-olds very much enjoy singing familiar songs. They quickly master new songs.

♪ They crave repetition and like to sing the same songs every day. The repetition of familiar songs helps create a kind of sonic structure and familiarity to the school day for these young students. The repetition also gives them a sense of mastery that builds self-esteem.

♪ These children like to accompany their songs with hand motions, dance, and other visual reinforcements such as pictures and photographs.

♪ Five- and six-year-olds love to dramatize songs, role-play, and take turns singing solo lines.

COMPOSITION

♪ Five- and six-year-olds love rhyming one-syllable words. This age is perfect for exploring lyric writing to familiar or invented melodies.

♪ Most five- and six-year-olds are ready and able to explore notes arranged in scales, both chromatic and diatonic. They can learn to sing scales and demonstrate the placement of pitches along a major scale using hand signs or physical representations of the sounds.

♪ When shown how to proceed, many five- and six-year-olds can create their own musical structures by working with basics such as pitch register, duration, and tempo.

COGNITIVE DEVELOPMENT

♪ At this age, some children are beginning to apply higher order logic in their examination of musical forms and structures. This means they may respond creatively to open-ended musical questions and challenges.

PERFORMANCE SKILLS

♪ Some children are very shy and do not want anyone to pay attention to the way they sound when they sing. They may withdraw and be self-conscious if they feel pressured to sing in class, so it's best to invite them but not to push. Their courage will develop with time and opportunity.

♪ At this age, some children are socially open. Those with outgoing or bold personalities might love to sing for family, classmates, or anyone who will listen. These children may excel when allowed to sing for their peers in class or in any group. Children with a natural interest in performing are old enough at this time to get involved in children's theater classes and local or school productions of musicals.

Seven to Eight Years

MUSICAL AWARENESS

♪ Second- and third-graders are sensitive to musical style. They tend to get very excited when the feel or mood of a predictable piece of music changes because they hear it performed with a different underlying rhythm. They like jazzy rhythms, rock rhythms, calypso and reggae rhythms—they look to rhythms for musical adventures that match their own high-wired energies. A nice activity is a family jam session during which you take a song everyone knows and rearrange it in a different time signature or with a new beat. This also helps children learn to exercise creative license.

PITCH DEVELOPMENT

♪ Primary-grade children may find ear training a bit more challenging than preschoolers do if they are enrolled in a class that makes them feel self-conscious or overly analytic. Competition instigated or tolerated by a music teacher at this age is a definite no-no. A good teacher for primary students is one who gets them so excited about making music that their inner critic automatically shuts off and their inner creator takes over. This kind of teacher knows kids like the back of her hand, chooses music they adore, and contains their naturally impulsive behavior while liberating their muse. If the children feel accepted and encouraged to take creative risks, they will sing more freely and their pitch development will continue to blossom. If they feel judged, they may clam up and try to fit in, or fade into the background.

♪ Primary-grade children are learning to match their voices to a pentatonic scale (five notes in a major scale, between *do* and *la*) and sing that scale in both ascending and descending order.

♪ Learning to sing notes in different intervals using solfège and corresponding hand signs helps six- to eight-year-olds sing all notes in tune. They learn to hear and match pitch very quickly at this stage, and the tunefulness lasts a lifetime.

♪ If a child is unable to modulate or match pitches at this stage, this is a prime time to begin very focused ear training with a qualified music instructor. If problems in pitch modulation and matching continue to present themselves, a concerned parent would be well advised to check his or her child's hearing and auditory processing with a speech-and-language or audiology specialist. Children can be born with impaired ability to discern sound or cognitively process what they are able to accurately hear. Chronic ear infections during childhood can but do not always contribute to this problem. Such infections may additionally result in a child developing resistance to listening because her ears have caused discomfort and educational/emotional stress over a prolonged period of time. Auditory processing problems can be helped and sometimes overcome with knowledgeable therapeutic intervention. Popular interventions include computer-based therapeutic treatments, specific exercises, and listening programs such as the one developed by Alfred Tomatis. More information is available in "Resources" at the back of this book.

RHYTHMIC DEVELOPMENT AND MOVEMENT

♪ Six- to eight-year-olds love to play around with rhythm on a wide variety of instruments. They are old enough to invent and make their own rhythm instruments out of found objects, junk, and odd hardware. See "Resources" for books on how to do this.

♪ Six- to eight-year-old children respond to rhythms with their entire bodies. Dance and movement reinforce their developing sense of rhythm and can be a meaningful and integral part of music instruction. Conversely, what they hear in a dance or movement class will transfer over to their general knowledge of music and reinforce their rhythmic abilities. In this way, all the arts feed each other.

INSTRUMENTAL DEVELOPMENT

♪ At this age, most children are ready and able to participate in private musical instruction or classes, as well as group experiences with music. They can apply their budding abilities and sensitivities to playing a musical instrument and taking instruction and guidance from a music teacher.

♪ Seven- and eight-year-olds are ready to learn about all kinds of musical instruments and musical ensembles. This is a great age to introduce them to the symphony orchestra as well as all kinds of world music ensembles.

♪ At this age, children may already know which instruments or instrument families they like. They are open to suggestions but value being asked about what they want to learn to play.

♪ Second- and third-graders who are able to complete homework assignments may be ready to knowingly commit to a practice routine and apply themselves to practicing their instrument at home in between lessons. Many can follow a daily and weekly routine, responding well to parent assistance, positive reinforcement, and encouragement from their teacher. Those who feel too confined by practice requirements may respond better to a more "process oriented" approach to lessons with less regard to goals and outcomes. Music for these children may be more about experiencing pleasure and broadening their horizons than developing excellent musical skills. If they like learning, their skill development will occur naturally.

♪ Many second- and third-graders are able to determine whether or not their skills are progressing. They can inform you when they feel their musical efforts sound good to them. They know when musical tasks are within their range of abilities or are beyond their reach. If you honor their self-evaluation of their instrumental progress and include them in decision making, they will feel more invested in their own progress and the outcomes of their lessons.

MUSIC THEORY

♪ Basic music theory is within the reach of some children in grades two and three. They are sometimes cognitively mature enough to understand the simple math and musical structures underlying most Western music. These students can learn to read, write, and play music with musical notation—a complex process because it requires the integration of auditory, visual, and kinesthetic skills.

♪ Second- and third-graders who experience a deficit in any of these cognitive areas may have difficulty learning music theory. These children will require adaptive teaching methods in order to progress. Please see the section in this book about learning styles for more information.

♪ The standardized expectations for children's understanding of music theory during grade three include reading, writing, performing, and understanding eighth, quarter, half, and whole notes; dotted notes; and common and 3/4 time signatures (aka *duple* and *triple* meters).

♪ Second- and third-graders are beginning to place notes in the context of a major scale on the musical staff, in the treble clef. Reading melodies written in the bass clef typically starts no sooner than grade four, when some children study instruments such as cello or contrabass whose music is all written in bass clef. Young students of piano may learn to read music in bass clef earlier than other children if they begin reading and playing music for two hands.

SINGING AND LEARNING SONGS

♪ Six- to eight-year-old children are beginning to gain control over their voices, and they have greater ability to sing softly and tunefully or with intentional volume and power. This means they can handle choral arrangements of songs that ask them to sing dynamically.

♪ Six- to eight-year-old children can sing different kinds of songs with leaders and followers, partners, and two-part arrangements. This means they can begin to handle choral arrangements of songs that ask them to sing a little simple harmony as well as in unison. They are old enough to participate in a primary-grade choir if one is available.

COMPOSITION

♪ The developmental increase in higher order conceptualization means six- to eight-year-olds can begin to manipulate the components of music into structures of their own design. Spatial, mathematically minded primary-grade students might create melodies with symmetric or intentionally asymmetric qualities. They may experiment with the way note durations and time signatures divide time.

♪ Verbally and emotionally expressive six- to eight-year-olds, given the right stimulation, are able to invent melodies that communicate feelings through shifts in melodic contour, tempo, and musical dynamics.

COGNITIVE DEVELOPMENT

♪ By the time a child is between six and eight years old, higher order logic has eclipsed pure listening and changed the way a child learns to make music. Older children begin thinking about what they hear and analyzing it in many regards. Children who have come to music making in infancy or very early childhood have an advantage. Even so, the window for learning music is still very much open at this time and throughout the primary grade years.

♪ Children taking lessons can give parents feedback about what they like and do not like about their lessons and related experiences. This feedback makes it possible for parents to make music lessons more positive and meaningful by working effectively with their child and teacher. If you listen closely and take time to reflect about your child's experiences and feelings before you commit to any course of change or action, you'll be able to discern whether your child is out of sorts, is having an off day, or has justifiable complaints about the lessons. If you are unsure, you can arrange to sit in on lessons for a while and form your own opinion of what's really going on.

♪ Six- to eight-year-olds are discovering who they are and dreaming a little about who they want to become. As they build musical skills, they unconsciously develop self-concepts based on their preferences, strengths, and weaknesses. Their peers notice what they do well and what they do poorly, and those areas of accomplishment or weakness dictate a certain amount of each child's self-esteem and social standing. Children who excel at making music are commonly thought of by peers as special, musical, and talented. Their dreams for the future may reflect this.

♪ When six- to eight-year-olds make music at school and home regularly, it can become a very healthy, central part of their lifestyle. It can help their health, both physical and mental, and give them focus, energetic release, and relaxation. Set in motion at this formative time, musicality will continue to enrich their lives, keeping them engaged in constructive endeavors that bring them together with other creative children.

PERFORMANCE SKILLS

♪ Musically motivated, outgoing seven- and eight-year-olds like to perform for fun and honor.

♪ Recitals are a normal event for children who study an instrument privately with a teacher who operates a music studio. Learning to perform requires special training and practice. It does not come naturally. Seven- and eight-year-olds benefit from parental support when handling this issue.

♪ Young musical prodigies begin to compete locally and nationally at this age.

♪ This is the perfect age to help children overcome stage fright and develop relaxation techniques to help them perform with greater confidence. Enrolling children in drama classes can help. Children's yoga classes may also prove beneficial for helping children develop the ability to breathe deeply and find their "center." Participation in class plays gives many second and third graders valuable experience learning to project, address the audience, and memorize their parts.

Questions, Answers, and More Questions

One of our strongest impulses as parents is to provide our children with answers to their questions. They ask, "Why?" and we want to respond with something better than, "Because." When our parents said, "Because," it just made us roll our eyes.

I developed the following section as a response to conversations I've had with parents who were encountering a host of issues regarding their children's musical development or study. It seems that resources for discussing such topics as problems with practice or how to go about selecting a musical instrument have been few and far between up to this point in time. In the pages that follow, I address a wide variety of such issues and offer reliable information as well as some personal opinions and recommendations with which readers may or may not agree. Every one of our children is unique, and our situations are special. So even if the fit is off here and there, I hope you'll use these chapters to attain a clearer sense of your own priorities. If you create a plan based on your own clear point of view, and you follow through, your children will know "where you are coming from" and why. They will not hear double messages, waffling, ambivalence, confusion.

So if you are facing a dilemma or feeling pressured to make a decision, how about buying yourself a little time in order to think things over? I recommend you stall the kids, then read the next chapters before you give your answer. I often resort to: "I'll think things over and get back to you as soon as I've made my decision." This is a response that most children will accept with a groan because they are relieved that, at least, you're taking them seriously. Then you'll have time to read on and mull over the possibilities late at night when you ought to be getting some much deserved sleep. This, of course, is what good parenting is all about.

When our parents said, "Because," it just made us roll our eyes.

Chapter 3
Pregnancy and Music

I'm nearly five months pregnant. Can my baby hear me if I sing or play music for him? Could playing music for him now make a difference in his level of musical ability when he is born?

The baby developing within you is just beginning to detect sounds. According to current research, fetuses can first sense sound between approximately 16 and 20 weeks. By the time babies reach 26 weeks in utero, their skin and possibly their ears are receptive to sounds and music. Lower frequencies (think cello, tuba, and male voices) are easiest to sense at first, and higher frequencies (think violin, flute, and female voices) seem to appeal most to babies after they are born.

Research has not yet proven that being exposed to music in utero makes babies more musically adept at birth, but many parents feel that music may reduce stress. For some, that is reason enough to make music during pregnancy. We know that fetal heart rates slow down nicely in utero when babies in utero experience music. But we do not know exactly what this means in terms of their future musical development. They are probably responding favorably to the music because they relax when they hear it. I imagine that anything that helps a developing fetus feel calm is worth doing. The fact that making music also benefits parents is nice, too.

Research has not yet proven that being exposed to music in utero makes babies more musically adept at birth, but many parents feel that music may reduce stress.

Back to baby. A baby's inner ears (cochleas) are developing during pregnancy. Some studies on pitch acquisition attribute having good pitch in part to one's cochlear maturity. The cochlea is the part of the ear that detects changes in sound frequencies, or pitches. Perhaps receiving musical stimulation in utero actually aids in the maturational process of the cochleas before birth. In any case, we can have fun making music during those incredible months before our babies are born. If we are coparenting, the prenatal musical process might even add new pleasure to our primary relationship. Anything we try together during those quiet days and nights of continual development has the potential to become special. As we say about so many things, why not try? It can't hurt.

I am not what you might think of as a "music person." I need quiet, and a lot of music just feels like noise to me. Can you please recommend some simple ways I can bring music into my life during pregnancy?

No need to go overboard. Just start with what comes naturally and do what feels reasonable. Sing to yourself as you do chores, and play pleasing, quiet recordings around the house and in the car. Perhaps this period of time will give you a chance to find a few new recordings you really like. Sounds like you might enjoy some gentle Baroque or early classical music, mellow jazz, or soft Brazilian jazz. You might also give a listen to Enya or some of the instrumental recordings from artist/producer George Winston and his label mates at Windham Hill. All these recordings have soothing qualities.

If you feel inclined to learn more about music at this time, I heartily recommend an educational audio series called *How to Listen to and Understand Great Music*, taught by professor Robert Greenberg and available through the Teaching Company. This brilliant educator, musician, and composer delivers well-planned lectures that take us through music history, helping us build music appreciation and knowledge. His recordings include brief examples of the music as he discusses it, ensuring we don't get lost.

You say you are not a music person. Yet you seem to hope that your baby will become one. Maybe you wish you knew how to play a musical instrument but lack the training or self-confidence. If you are game, why not try something simple and keep your expectations within reason? There is no shame in taking beginning lessons as an adult. If this option interests you, I'd suggest you sign up for four lessons with a kind teacher who will get you started on some sort of gateway instrument that sounds good right away. Percussion, recorder, harp, and folk guitar all give the new musician some gratification right off the bat.

Some moms join informal, community-based singing groups such as Mothersong in Santa Cruz, California. Some sing in choirs at places of worship. A weekly song gathering can feel very nurturing and good during pregnancy. So if singing holds some appeal for you, take a quick look in the calendar section of your local paper. There should be a couple of fun choices to check out. Plus, involvement in this kind of activity will probably bring new, like-minded friends into your life.

If you exercise, do so while you listen to music. All that healthy breathing, relaxing, circulating, and taking care of yourself will be good for your baby, too. The side benefits might include a nice endorphin release and a righteous desire to eat cheesecake or ice cream later.

On another note, let's discuss environmental music and your developing baby. It sounds as though you are not one of those people who enjoy horror films, action adventures, or thrillers. The music in such theatrical releases is played at such a high volume and is meant to build fear or to shock the audience. The spikes in volume can make your heart race or skip a beat. I would encourage expectant mothers to refrain from listening to distressing sound tracks like these during the last trimester of pregnancy. Anything that raises your stress is bound to do the same thing to your baby. Since the fetal heart rate decreases while babies in utero listen to soothing music, it follows that the state you'd want to induce is one of calm listening instead of fist clenching and teeth gritting. Same thing goes for rock concerts. Volume levels are so high that your baby could feel alarmed and unable to screen out the sound. My opinions are based purely on common sense and personal experience, but perhaps someday science will bear them out.

Technically speaking, studies show that fetuses are most receptive to low-frequency vibrations at first. If you are playing recordings, you are probably best off selecting some music with a strong beat and audible bass parts (two 1981 recordings featuring the late bassist Jaco Pastorius come to mind). I'll bet babies in utero would also really respond to Barry White, but I do not suppose *that* will ever be scientifically researched.

Some expectant parents feel so strongly about introducing music in utero that they place a tape recorder near the mom's belly or get special equipment for that purpose.

Some expectant parents feel so strongly about introducing music in utero that they place a tape recorder near the mom's belly or get special equipment for that purpose. Baby Plus is a prenatal music listening system designed to put the music and sound as close to baby as possible. Created by developmental psychologist Dr. Brent Logan, the system comes with a belt that contains tiny audio speakers and a cassette player. Mom wears this over her belly each morning and night, playing one of 16 tapes that feature rhythmic sounds resembling a mother's heartbeat. Dr. Logan believes his system promotes fetal intellectual development while attuning baby to sound sensation. At this point in history, we might all be considered informal researchers in this field.

At the end of the day, whatever you decide to do with music should be pleasurable and leave you feeling either rested or energized and inspired. Allow your heart to be your guide—for both you and baby.

I have two left feet and hope my baby will be spared a similar fate! Is there anything a mother-to-be can do during pregnancy to help her baby acquire some natural rhythm?

First let's examine that phrase. What is "natural rhythm?" The term really refers to how effortless someone else's rhythmic talent seems to a person who feels rhythmically challenged. Whether or not it's *natural* is another story.

What do we mean by *natural?* If we mean an intrinsic quality that presents itself from birth, then a baby who has regularly experienced rocking or dancing rhythms in utero might seem to have natural rhythm. It makes sense—rhythm has been wired into that baby's brain and being from the get-go. But rocking and bouncing your baby around to the steady beat during the first couple years of life might have the same effect. Electric swings and doorway bouncing seats certainly have also gotten a lot of infants and toddlers moving to the beat.

Funny how we have to resort to rhythmic motion to calm babies down during the fussy 4–6 P.M. hours! Ever notice how parents of infants tend to shift their weight in time from side to side when they are standing in a checkout line at the store? Children naturally calm themselves with rhythm when they are old enough. We've all seen how toddlers will rock back and forth on the floor or on a rocking horse to soothe themselves.

As children get a bit older, it's easy to see those natural rhythms finding new forms of expression. It's not unusual to observe toddlers mindlessly playing a short sequence of steady beats by tapping a box or a toy. They can shake rattles to the beat, too. Some children love rhythm so much that they are drawn to playing instruments for fun. Others are awesome dancers even at three years of age. The months from birth through the time a baby begins to walk present parents with a wonderful opportunity to play and move rhythmically with infants. Programs such as Music Together and Gymboree provide families with stimulating, developmentally appropriate classes that nurture rhythmic ability and make everyone smile. For lucky you, this time is just around the bend!

But let's be clear. No newborn comes into the world ready to tap dance. Rhythmic ability emerges as rhythmic skills develop in children during early childhood and beyond. Chances are good that babies who hear a lot of music in their homes and who are rocked to the beat are most likely to become accustomed to hearing and feeling rhythm. In this sense, parents have been unintentionally giving their babies rhythmic training since the beginning of human existence. I ask you— can rhythm possibly get any more natural than that?

For now, during your pregnancy, you might consider enrolling in a dance class for your own fun, or joining a drumming class or circle led by someone supportive of beginners. You are the one you can take care of now, before the baby is born. I encourage you to treat yourself to rhythmic play in your own life before

your daily schedule becomes punctuated by the unpredictable, syncopated pattern of diaper change, feeding, diaper change, feeding, nap, diaper change, feeding, nap, diaper change, feeding, diaper change, feeding, nap! It's time to kick up your heels. As Bobby McFerrin sings, "Don't worry. Be happy."

I cannot get my husband to sing. He just refuses. His music teacher in junior high told him to "mouth the words" and he has been doing it ever since. When I sing to myself (which I do constantly) he pokes fun, but I want to sing. I am excited to be having this baby, and I want him to sing to the baby, too. My dad always sang to me and I still love the sound of his voice. How can I get my shower-singing man to gain a little self-confidence?

First, you might tell your husband that his baby in utero is more likely to respond to a male voice than a female one, and ask him to hum a little tune for his baby. Humming can be less threatening to the nervous singer than a song with lyrics. You might also let him know that it will calm and please the baby. Maybe a little music from his lips will make you feel romantic toward him. Tell him about a boy you had a crush on in high school who sang with a band. Muse out loud about what that boy might be doing now. If it doesn't get him to sing, at least it should get him to chuckle.

Second, you can be a stealthy music operative. Plant singing into the course of regular conversation by singing to your husband as part of your end of the dialogue. Maybe he'll respond in kind.

If you're taking a car trip, you might see if you can get him to join you singing old campfire songs. If at all possible for everyone's sake, avoid "99 Bottles of Beer" and "John Jacob Jingleheimer Schmidt." Learn from my mistakes.

At just the right moment, you might ask him to sing you songs he remembers from childhood. If you want to get very resourceful, you could drag out his favorite recordings from high school and get him singing along with them. Eventually, he will figure out that singing feels good once he stops worrying about how he sounds. The more he sings and sees that you like the sound of it, the more often he'll sing. I know. It took my husband about three years to make a peep. Now he sings to our boy once in a while without giving it a thought, and we all have a good time together with music. But it took patience, cunning, and perseverance on my part to be sure, all well worth the effort.

Paying your partner genuine compliments seems to help a lot. A simple "That sounds good, honey" can go a long, long way. You could tell him you like his tone, or praise his delivery. Request a special song. You might even give him the gift of guitar lessons or concert tickets, or take him to a music club for a romantic evening. One note of caution: be prepared for success. One friend of mine started taking guitar lessons, ostensibly to play music with his two young children. Now he goes to class twice a week and collects nice instruments, and his wife has begun hiding the credit cards!

If you think you can coax one song out of your partner, I recommend you do it with the tape recorder to capture the moment. If he'll let you make a tape of him singing a lullaby for the baby, then you can play it for the baby when daddy is keeping mum.

My partner and I want to choose music to play during our baby's birth. Do you have any recommendations?

These days it's easy to bring music into your childbirth experience. Doctors, nurses, and midwives are happy to listen while they work, and the right music will help you relax when you need to rest and muster your energy. Many delivery rooms and birthing centers are already prepared for playing music during childbirth. It's wise to check first.

The job of arranging the music for the birth is a great way to get your mind or your partner's off worries and into something positive near the delivery date. It's also a great job for a friend who wants to help out. Being the delivery deejay makes a good channel for nervous energy during long stretches of labor! Of course we've all heard stories of

anything from Hawaiian ukulele to Nigerian dance and griot society drumming! Anything that creates wonder for you and your child together will be fun to explore further. The greater the variety, the better for learning

In addition to seeking inspiration through entertainment, you can also make your home and family life more musical in ways large and small. Here are some suggestions that are easy to put into practice.

- Integrate singing into your daily lives. Sing to and with your children just for fun. You can use cassettes to get started if that helps you build a repertoire and some confidence. Share your old favorite songs. Dust off some silly songs and camp songs for the car.

Songs that feature repetition such as "Bingo" and "Old MacDonald" help young children memorize the words and melodies. For slightly older children, call-and-repeat patterns or call-and-response parts are perfect. They give children a chance to hear how their part goes ahead of time. Some examples include "You Can't Get to Heaven," "I Am a Pizza," and "Yellow Submarine." Rhyming songs such as "Baby Beluga," "Fooba Wooba John," and "Rock around the Clock" hold special appeal for children in grades one through three. If you wish to purchase a recording of children's songs, there are hundreds to choose from. Listening online or in stores will help you decide which ones to buy. For suggestions, please read the list of recommended recordings in the "Resources" chapter of this book.

- Introduce singing into some of the little transitions and tasks that take place every day. Relaxation songs and bedtime songs can fit nicely into soothing family routines. Rhymes and ditties have helped many parents get their kids into healthy routines. For instance, Woody Guthrie's song "Pick It Up" really gets five-year-olds into helping clean up after themselves. And toddlers take pleasure in pretending to take care of their pearly whites with the ever-popular "Brush Your Teeth."

- Preschoolers go crazy over electronic musical toys, miniature electric pianos, and moveable musical blocks with flashing lights and sophisticated programming. The Fisher-Price Smart Symphonies is an ideal example for babies. It allows very young children to trigger and sequence music with a single touch. Babies become familiar with popular childhood and classical melodies while they're playing.

- Get your child a keyboard-style synthesizer with preprogrammed melodies she can play independently in the backseat while you are on the go. The V-Tech Little Smartie has many intriguing features and is built to survive! Some synths teach children to identify melodies, then have the children play along by pressing the correct keys as they light up in the right order.

- Every now and again, start an informal family jam session using both melodic and unpitched percussion instruments. Rainy afternoons and family times after a meal are perfect opportunities for making music together. Keep a basket of simple rhythm instruments such as drums, tambourines, sticks, and bells on hand for these occasions. These allow young music makers to hone their motor skills while they play simple rhythms.

- Rent old movies of Broadway musicals and watch them together. Choose your favorite numbers and sing them.

- Study a musical instrument or join a choir, and practice when your children are at home so they can hear you making an effort. When you demonstrate what effective practice looks and sounds like, your children may simply accept it as a part of everyday life.

- Take your child to hear live performances of music at local cafés, festivals, concerts, and theaters. Beforehand, when possible, help your youngster become familiar with the musical style or even some of the melodies she will hear during the live performance. This deepens her awareness of and interest in the music. For instance, if you're going to a musical play, get the soundtrack or the film version a couple weeks before the show, and listen to it at home. If you're attending a classical performance, play her the pieces she'll hear and listen for the most prevalent themes together. When possible and appropriate, make the connections between live performance and home video.

• Enroll your child in classes that include music as a secondary art form. Dance lessons, art lessons, yoga classes, or creative movement where music is played will expand your child's musical horizons indirectly.

• When possible, share your child's favorite recordings with teachers and child-care providers. Ask them to play the music during the times when they supervise your child.

• Help your child give copies of his or her favorite recordings to friends as gifts. This is a meaningful way to teach your child to share artistic values.

Shirley Temple

My partner and I are expecting our third child. Our firstborn is already eight, and our middle child is almost four. Lately I've been seeing all kinds of ads for early childhood music classes. I get the impression that if children do not start making music at three, they're sure to miss the boat. Can any kid learn to do sing like Shirley Temple if they start while they're still in diapers? Am I too late?

It's true that the earlier children begin to make music, the easier and more natural their musical expression seems to develop. But you can take heart and relax. Children can get involved in music at any age, although starting before age six seems to yield the best results. Shirley Temple's mother, Gertrude, gave Shirley an early start by introducing her to music, art, and nature even before she was born. In 1934 she was quoted as saying, "Perhaps this prenatal preparation helped make Shirley what she is."

Shirley Temple's mother, Gertrude, gave Shirley an early start by introducing her to music, art, and nature even before she was born.

Shirley Temple seems to have had all her musical ducks in a row right from first—rhythm, pitch, melodic memory, physical coordination. She possessed every kind of musical sensitivity and made musicality appear effortless. But her mother had such a strong hand in helping Shirley discover and nurture all those sensitivities and talents from the beginning of life; we can only say Shirley's phenomenal talent was "natural" insofar as mothering is natural! One key to her success was probably that she started feeling, hearing, and making music long before she was old enough to doubt herself or question the value of it all.

To understand your own children's musical development, please look over the stages of musical development in this book. The descriptions will help you gain a clearer picture of what children are expected to be able to do, and how and when it is generally thought that they can acquire specific musical skills.

Since becoming musical is not a predictable process, how fair is it for parents to regard it as some sort of achievement race? Everyone's course and timing is unique. We tend to make so much of early accomplishment. In fact, becoming a musical person is bound to be rewarding at all levels of achievement and at any age or stage! Being best is not always what's best for a child. Any child prodigy will tell you that in some regards, the experience is far from idyllic. Exceptionally gifted children may find they have a hard time fitting in with other children their own ages. Balancing and developing life skills and abilities that lie outside of their area of giftedness presents prodigies with very real emotional challenges. Parenting such a child can and perhaps should become a full-time occupation for anyone who wishes their child to develop a healthy lifestyle and a secure sense of self and belonging.

Musical vocalizations and call-and-response games are a natural part of how infants acquire spoken language.

How can I tell if my infant is musical?

Signs of musical sensitivity have been scientifically noted in infants, but true abilities become more apparent over time. For instance, when we pay close attention to infants, we see how they respond to music by vocalizing, waving their arms, or turning their heads toward the source of the sound. We might actually hear their early attempts at singing.

Musical vocalizations and call-and-response games are a natural part of how infants acquire spoken language. They experiment with sounds and pitches all the time. Babies raise and lower their voices to express excitement, stress, pain, and pleasure. Sometimes they modulate their voices just for fun. When your new baby comes, you will know what to look and listen for. The best way to know what your baby can do is to play little vocalization games even in the first month of life. Imitate Baby's sounds and watch a look of delight cross her face. Listen closely and see if she tries to imitate you!

When they are old enough, infants begin to imitate specific pitches. As far as we know, the cochlea continues to develop over time, and improved pitch perception goes along with it. So it's important not to confuse the issue of whether or not someone is "born" with talent with the issue of when musical "talent" emerges. Children are capable of achieving musicality under beneficial circumstances when the time is right. Talent is potential that dwells within us all. The goal is to cultivate and express it. Undoubtedly, your infant is innately musical and you will notice it when you draw it out.

An early childhood music and movement program just opened in my neighborhood, and I was thinking of going with my three-year-old. Do you believe that these classes are worth the money?

Only you can decide whether a particular program is worthwhile for members of your family, but in general, early childhood music and movement classes are extremely beneficial for children; plus, parents get the side benefit of sharing inspirational quality time away from home making music.

Research tells us that between the ages of birth and six, children acquire basic musical intelligence with the greatest ease. Their ears are open, their hands will try anything, their bodies respond to melody and a bouncy beat. It's all a game. When shared with a parent, these classes become learning labs for all kinds of new skills—physical, social, emotional, and musical!

Before the age of six, children find music pleasurable. They sing for fun. They do not think about what they are doing very much. Between the ages of six and eleven, children become more intellectual, conceptual, and critical in their thinking. They are still quite receptive to learning music at this stage, but their ability to think abstractly can actually complicate the process. As children mature, they begin to look before they leap and think before they act. They take pride in newfound abilities to analyze their circumstances. Basic skills such as hearing and matching pitches in tune are given secondary status when children are more curious about related issues such as music theory or popular culture. Later, when we add the social and psychological component of peer acceptance and pressure, the pace of learning to make music can be affected.

During the upper grades of elementary school and beyond, the act of making music most commonly takes place in a class or a social group. Fitting in becomes a primary goal. So learning to express oneself musically requires self-confidence or social risk taking. This is when a lot of children start to clam up or sit out. Unless musical skills and self-esteem have already been instilled, this is when parents typically hear musically self-deprecating statements from their children. "I can do that" turns into "I'm not as good as So-and-So." A young person who would once sing a song with abandon now contemplates whether to open her mouth in music class. The potential for learning still exists, but a child's shaky self-esteem can thwart the learning process. Only playing guitar is generally considered cool. A few chords and strums, and your big kid can acquire new social status.

That early childhood music class could be more important than you think. It might open your child's heart and soul to music and get him on a musical path when he is wide open to learning. Later on in the upper

Between the ages of six and eleven, children become more intellectual, conceptual, and critical in their thinking.

Many famous guitar players didn't pick up a guitar until they were in high school.

elementary grades, if he has pursued a music education and begun to play an instrument, he will begin to think of himself as musically capable. His self-esteem and confidence will protect him from becoming an unmusical teen. Those years between birth and six hold great potential for shaping your child's future sense of himself.

Interesting new brain research on adolescent development gives all parents a reason to hope that children who missed the benefits of early musical training can still learn to play an instrument. It explains why some musical greats did not begin tapping into their musical potential until they reached adolescence. Many famous guitar players didn't pick up a guitar until they were in high school. The adolescent brain goes through a tremendous growth spurt equaled only by that in early childhood. To learn more, please read *The Primal Teen* by Carol Strauch. However, once a child takes a musical path, his potential for learning never decreases

When I was a kid, we listened to whatever our parents put on the stereo—not to "children's music." I didn't understand it all, but I liked some of it, especially the big Motown hits. What is all the buzz about "age appropriate" music?

There are two popular points of view regarding music composed and recorded specifically for children. Some people think it's dippy and musically simplistic, and that the lyrics can be condescending. Others think it's socially appropriate, developmentally relevant, and safer for young ears than some of the pop slop and sexy stuff available on mainstream radio. Why make an extreme choice one way or the other? Perhaps Raffi, the Beatles, and No Doubt can all contribute to your child's developing musicality. I recommend voting the issues, not the party. Good music of any kind is worthwhile, and tasteless music is an annoying waste of time. It doesn't matter who exactly the music was intended to reach if it affects your child in a positive way.

Children can enjoy any kind of music they hear, from Broadway to reggae, if it's got a beat or a mood they relate to and includes a catchy melody or captivating lyrics. As long as the music is free from blatantly or subliminally sexual or hostile content, it may be considered developmentally appropriate—that is, in line with children's emotional and social needs. This is not to say that children do not relate to hostile or angry music. They have those feelings too. It's a matter of what we wish to emphasize as valuable.

Many of my upper elementary students absolutely love punk music. And a number of elementary-age girls adopt the sexualized fashions and behaviors they see on MTV and VH1. Oddly, they do so during what is known as the latency period of childhood psychological development, a time when sexuality naturally goes underground in the young psyche. During a stage when young girls typically reject boys in favor of friendships with other girls (most often seen in grades two through six), they are concurrently learning to flaunt their bodies like the divas on television. This clashing of media and mind permeates so many schools today, unconsciously setting a norm for playful sexualized behavior that has no anchor in childhood psychology. Kids send and receive double messages during a stage in their lives when actual sexual contact would be not only repulsive to them but could be very damaging as well.

Of course, how any parent handles these issues is a matter of personal taste and belief. At the end of the day, it's up to us to decide what our kids can and should handle, and to help them make sense out of the music and the values they encounter. We owe it to them to make conscious choices about the music they hear when they are little. When they are big, it's up to us to stay current, ask questions, and question pop wisdom.

If you are interested in introducing your children to music that pleases audiences of many ages, some styles and bands that typically go over very well during the elementary school years include The Beatles, swing jazz, old Motown hits, '50s rock and doo-wop tunes, and selected pop hits from the past four decades. My elementary school students

At the end of the day, it's up to parents to decide what kids can and should handle, and to help them make sense out of the music they encounter in their environment.

have brought in everything from Elvis and disco to Men at Work to share with their peers in my music classes. A few rare students have shared a favorite sonata or concerto. No one has brought in opera. Yet.

Popular and classical music aside, let's discuss what is commonly called children's music. Children thoroughly enjoy music written specifically for their age group as long as it's worthwhile both lyrically and musically. Many talented composers and performers work in the field of children's music. Just as we have our favorite love songs, kids have their favorite pet songs and silly songs. They can be quite comforted or intrigued by lyrics about things they experience such as riding a bike, losing a friend, or taking care of an animal. They like to sing about the earth. They learn about heroes and history through folk songs. You may not want to listen to that music for entertainment, but they might. If your child has his own boom box and some kids' recordings, just add headphones and everyone's happy.

Some songs for children have social, even therapeutic value. Certain songs impart ideals. Others help children make sense of their personal

Some songs for children have social, even therapeutic value. Certain songs impart ideals. Others help children make sense of their personal experiences.

experiences. Meaningful lyrics can provide children with new vocabulary to describe their feelings. Some songs help them recognize the universality of what they thought were unique experiences such as being angry at one's sibling or feeling embarrassed over a mistake. Other songs for children boost their verbal ability and trigger their imaginations through wordplay, rhymes, and poetry. Topical songs

about everything from science to spelling can also make academic learning more fun. So why not give "children's" music a chance?

Music that has been recorded in keys that are compatible for children's singing voices can also contribute to their acquisition of some musical skills. Studies show that children develop a sense of pitch and the ability to sing along when they hear songs sung in a range that matches their own voices. Recordings that feature children as the vocalists, like many of those available from Music for Little People, accomplish this very well. For a listing of recommended singer-friendly recordings, please see "Resources."

Chapter 5

Jump-Starting Your Child's Music Education

Since my seven-year-old attends a school that doesn't have a music education program, it's up to me to get her started. How and where do I begin?

Start by trusting that sometimes, when parents do nothing more than teach children to notice and appreciate music as a normal part of life, the children fall in love with music and become musicians anyway. Although benign neglect is not the ideal musical parenting approach, many successful musicians have come from that kind of upbringing. Some children are so wired for making music that a little encouragement is enough to get them started. Sounds like you would like to offer your daughter a lot more, and that you are willing to take steps to educate yourself first. She is a very lucky person.

If you'll read the description in "Parents As Musical Partners" of musical development as a braid, you'll get some practical ideas for stimulating your child's musicality at home and out in the world of the performing arts. To formulate a plan for music education, how about starting with a parent-child discussion about what music your child enjoys the most? Right there you are giving her encouragement to pay attention to and follow her musical instincts. Next, of course, you'll want to find out what kinds of instruction and enrichment programs are available in your area.

Before you decide which instructor or program best suits your daughter, it would help to have a clear idea of her strengths and challenges. Take her learning style into account. Every child can learn to make music, but each one learns a little differently, as we will explore in the next chapter. Understanding your child's unique qualities will make it easier to select a suitable teacher and supply that teacher with insights about his or her new student.

To find a teacher in your area, begin by asking around. Consult your local grapevine before you thumb through the yellow pages. Chat with folks about what teachers, classes, and lessons their children have enjoyed (or not). You may hear of someone teaching who does not advertise. This is often the case with well-established private instructors. Their studios are full of students, and they do not need to look for more. If you want to enroll your child in lessons there, it's important to call and get on the waiting list, if one exists.

If you want to enroll your child in a method-based program such as Suzuki, Yamaha, Kindermusik, or Music Together, you can often find those classes advertised in a local parenting magazine or in the phone book.

Many music stores also offer lessons or refer customers to favorite private teachers. The managers usually know which teachers are popular with kids and parents. You can also find programs, teachers, and musical events listed on the Internet. Many small programs even have their own websites. Search under "music lessons" and the name of your town or county. In addition, sometimes professional organizations for music teachers such as the Music Educator's National Conference or Music Teacher's National Association list their members or give referrals online. These resources could provide you with some information about each teacher's training.

If you take several weeks to explore your options, your search for the right class or teacher can be exhaustive without becoming exhausting. You and your child can arrive at a decision feeling secure and relaxed.

Parent-run arts groups have made a world of difference in bringing music education back to elementary schools.

For tips on evaluating prospective teachers, see "Music Teachers and Programs."

One more way to plan and implement your child's music education is to volunteer for your school's arts committee. Parent-run arts groups have made a world of difference in bringing music education back to elementary schools. Parent advocacy for basic music education at school has, in many instances helped make music education available to all children, not only to those whose parents can afford it.

Once my daughter is enrolled in a music class, how will I tell if it's right for her?

It's great to see your child smiling at the end of a music lesson. Even better to hear her practicing at home. But is that enough information for you to know how she is doing in her music lessons? Of course not! But it's a good start.

For an eye-opening look at what music educators believe each child is capable of learning at every grade level, please look over the national standards for music education on the Music Educators National Conference website (www.menc.org). It's surprising just how much musical potential children possess.

Children suffer when parents take a one-size-fits-all approach to choosing teachers

Watch any class at recess, and you'll see every kind of learner. Some kids just have to move around, and they change tasks frequently. Others focus on a single task without looking up until the bell rings. Some children play alone or with one friend, content with peace and quiet. Others talk everyone else's ears off and are always running with a pack of kids. All these traits suggest prevalent learning styles, and those styles play key roles in how children will fare in music lessons and classes. Congratulations on thinking ahead about how your children's styles could require different teaching approaches. Children sometimes suffer when parents take a one-size-fits-all approach to choosing teachers or allow convenience to dominate their choice of teachers, settings, and lesson times.

Heredity plays a powerful role in determining how we learn. This is particularly evident with disabilities such as Attention Deficit Disorder (A.D.D.) and dyslexia. It sounds as if your children may have inherited very different learning styles. So as you puzzle out how to get your children into the right lessons, it might help to reflect on your own early learning experiences; try to remember what worked for you and what didn't. Compare yourself to your child to see if there are stylistic similarities. Your partner's early experiences are also just as valid. A nice long conversation about *yourselves* as students could help the two of you decide what to look for in teachers or approaches for your kids.

It's also productive to look beyond genetics to the environments in which our children live and go to school when we want to understand how they function. The food they eat plays a role as well. Sugar often gives kids bursts of energy that burn out and leave them drooping. Allergies can impair learning; most common are dust, dander, pollen, dairy, and wheat allergies. Vision and hearing play important roles too. Every aspect of your children's physical well-being factors into their ability to concentrate and make progress.

A search over the Internet and a quick look through "Resources" in this book will point you toward informative books and websites about learning styles, learning disabilities, and learning profiles. If you take a little time to look through the current literature, you may recognize your own family's learning-style patterns. Perhaps your sister's math phobia could have its family roots in a spatial learning disability that led everyone in your family in 1900 to tease your great grandmother about getting lost a lot. These things rarely come out of the blue. Brother's gifted delivery of toasts at weddings may have started in 1700 with some ancient relative whose job title was town crier.

Once you get a handle on your children's prevalent learning styles, you'll be better able to evaluate which kinds of musical instruction and teachers will allow them to put their best hands and feet forward. All of us employ a variety of sensory systems to gather, comprehend, remember, and apply information. These include five learning modalities: visual, grapho-motoric, auditory, kinesthetic, and experiential (aka multisensory). Each one functions like a channel that can receive, process, retain, coordinate, and send information. When a channel works well, we learn and create well through its modality. For example, if we are auditorily oriented, we learn by listening; we remember what we hear, and reinforce and expand upon our learning through oral communication such as talking and singing.

Once you get a handle on your children's prevalent learning styles, you'll be better able to evaluate which kinds of musical instruction will allow them to put their best hands and feet forward.

When a channel works poorly, we use it and get confused, or we do not use it much at all. We may come to depend entirely upon the other channels or modalities because they work better for us. The less we use our weaker channels, the more we depend on the strong ones. So it would seem to follow that the best modalities get better and, to quote the great Billie Holiday, "...the weak ones fade." If we know which learning styles our children experience as strong and weak, we can help their teachers put the former to work in service of the latter. Many profiles of learning styles are available for free on the Internet with a simple search for the key words *learning styles inventory*.

The following descriptions of music students may help us imagine what each learning style might look like in our own children and how these might play out in music lessons. Perhaps this chapter's section titled "Your Kinesthetic and Tactile Child" on page 78 will address some of the qualities you've noticed in your very active son.

Your Visual Child

If your child is a visual learner, she remembers what she sees and reads perhaps even better than what she hears. She likes lists, posters, and photographs—anything that lets her feast her eyes on ideas.

A visual child talks about "seeing" when she understands something. If you ask her to describe a feeling or explain an idea, she paints a picture for you with words. She is sensitive to colors, details, perspectives, design features, the way her world looks.

As a music student, this child will respond favorably to the use of visual aids. She'll do well with a music teacher who illustrates her points on a chalk, felt, or dry-erase board. Note cards, flash cards, and worksheets will help her grasp ideas and commit them to memory. She'll want sheet music, chord charts, diagrams, and lyrics in front of her when she's making music. This child needs to write her practice regimen down at the time of her music lesson so she can review and follow the plan later.

Children with some spatial reasoning ability and a strong visual style have the easiest time learning to read music. These children benefit from their knack for gauging physical attributes such as size, shape, and distance, remembering where things are located in relation to other things, and translating symbols into meanings. Learners with weak visual and spatial skills can improve them with specific exercises and activities available through educational therapy.

Encourage your visual child to keep a notebook with songs and other music she gathers on loose-leaf or music paper. This binder can be her own personal songbook. She might even like to illustrate it, making collages, charts, or diagrams to reinforce her lessons.

Children with some spatial reasoning ability and a strong visual style have the easiest time learning to read music.

She may also enjoy watching musical films and music education videos. She can get a lot from reading picture books of illustrated songs, biographies of great composers and musicians, and from reading nonfiction books about the history of music. Songbooks with scopes and photographs from Hollywood films and Broadway musicals might really get her jazzed.

Your Auditory Child

Auditory children are often labeled early in life as musically talented. (Strong auditory ability becomes evident as early as the first months of life when babies listen to and copy what they hear.) The auditory child typically understands and remembers what he hears. You can ask him to handle four or five tasks, and he'll do them all in the correct sequence without writing a list. He remembers people's phone numbers, lyrics to countless songs, stories—anything he has received while listening. He does best in classes taught by lively speakers and enriched by multimedia presentations. Teachers with monotonous voices put him to sleep.

Some auditory children are avid conversationalists, but others save their talk, preferring to listen instead. Your auditory child might read in a whisper to himself because the sound of his own voice reinforces the meaning of what he is reading. He might be a hummer, someone who creates sound for his own pleasure. He probably loves musical and theatrical presentations of every kind. He might avoid writing things down in favor of remembering information after hearing it repeated once or twice. He may get himself to memorize information by saying it out loud. (Three verbal repetitions of information can really make the ideas stick!) When cramming for a test, mnemonic devices such as acronyms and funny sentences help an auditory child retrieve rote information.

The auditory child typically excels at what Dr. Edwin Gordon calls audiation, the act of imagining music without actually hearing it played by musicians. Audiation means one can put musical sounds and ideas together in one's mind, vividly imagining how they sound if played by musicians with instruments. Auditory learners have the easiest time accomplishing audiation, so naturally an auditory child sings to himself and improvises melodies. He may be able to hear a piece of music once or twice, then sing or play the melody on his instrument without reading so much as a note of music.

The ease with which your auditory child learns music by ear can make understanding written notation and music theory seem like hard work by comparison.

An auditory child learns to play music quickly because he hears and remembers how things are supposed to sound. He is far less dependent on sheet music than his visual peers. His teacher can sing or play a melody, and he is able to repeat it effortlessly. He memorizes music by singing or playing it several times. Once he has committed the music to memory, he may disregard the printed sheet music and veer off into improvisations just to keep his ears happily challenged.

The ease with which your auditory child learns music by ear can make analyzing and understanding written notation and music theory seem like hard work by comparison. Many auditory musicians never bother to learn to read music at all. This can become a stumbling block later in life should this child ever want to audition for an orchestra or work as a studio musician. Reading music well is a prerequisite to many kinds of musical work. It *is* a prerequisite for college-level music education.

To help your auditory child become a well-rounded musician, it's wise to pair him with a teacher who engages him through listening and playing music by ear, then teaches him the visual aspects of music by associating signs and symbols with auditory reinforcement. Some of the best multimodal approaches for teaching the auditory child to read music include naming notes out loud while reading them; playing with and placing textured notes of an oversized staff using materials such as Velcro, sandpaper, or carpet notes; learning to sing with solfège (*do re mi* . . .) while making hand signs for the pitches; playing music card games; and, best of all, learning to write music down.

An auditory child may like inventing or improvising music. Any auditory learner can easily be coaxed to compose a melody. The best teacher for your auditory child is the one who helps him express his creativity through musical improvisation, then shows him how to write his musical ideas down and read them back; this ties the auditory, grapho-motoric, and visual systems together. When your auditory child can write down what he hears and plays, reading other music will naturally follow.

Some children have the auditory equivalent of a photographic memory. Learning specialists refer to this ability as "auditory sequential memory." This means they can perceive and interpret sounds accurately, retaining them in memory in the exact order they originally occurred. In addition to memorizing melodies and lyrics, these children are probably also great at remembering lists, stories, and anything related to series of symbols such as numbers. They may be able to listen to a CD, then transcribe an instrumental part onto paper and play it back precisely. This kind of auditory talent can also predispose a child to becoming a successful actor and entertainer, reciting lines or running monologues from memory.

A child with extra auditory *and* kinesthetic-tactile prowess may develop the ability to play more than one instrument well. If this applies to your child, you might consider looking into instruments that are related such as clarinet and saxophone, guitar and bass, drums and percussion. Some musicians are able to cross over between musical families quite well, although this is less common.

It is also great to introduce an auditory child to music from around the world. Listening to the wildly varying time signatures and scales, he'll acquire an appreciation for musical structures other than those he hears on pop radio. He may choose to incorporate these sounds in his own playing and composition later in life.

This kid is a good candidate for a garage band when he's old enough; jamming with other musical children tends to bring out the best in kids who have musical ears. They learn to collaborate and discover the joy of playing together in a groove.

Your Visual Child Who Is Not Auditory

It's possible for children to demonstrate adequate strength in a number of learning styles simultaneously. These are the luckiest students by far because they can soak up information so many ways. But visual learners are not necessarily strong auditory learners. Many people become either strongly auditory or strongly visual by the time they reach junior high school, perhaps from the "use it or lose it" aspect of our brains. So unless a predominantly visual child is sufficiently challenged to develop her auditory skills as well, she may become dependent on the printed page in order to play music. This describes many of us as adults.

Many visually oriented musicians feel nervous about improvising music, even a tiny bit. Dependent on those little black notes and straight lines, visual-only musicians often refrain from trying to play anything "off the top of their heads." This can lead to having poor self-esteem if we see ourselves as less creative than musicians who can pull a melody out of thin air. It can also be uncomfortable in social situations when party-goers ask us to lead or accompany a song without the benefit of sheet music. It's much more pleasant to be able to vamp some chords on the piano while others croon away the night.

Which approach helps the visually oriented student strengthen her auditory processing and auditory memory? One that includes plenty of vocal and instrumental ear training, listening activities, and musical improvisation. Such an approach reaches beyond standard piano lessons in which the teacher leads the student through a book of short exercises and scales. The best teacher or program will help your auditorily challenged child develop useful skills and confidence through activities such as imitating musical phrases by ear, making up melodies, and noting and describing what she hears the teacher play. The teacher will help your daughter internalize music and begin to audiate. The hope is that your visual child will begin to feel as though she "owns" the music, rather than borrowing it from the printed page.

The hope is that your visual child will begin to feel as though she "owns" the music, rather than borrowing it from the printed page.

If your child has an actual auditory processing disorder (A.P.D.), the specific qualities of the problem can and should be diagnosed by a speech and language professional with excellent training in A.P.D. Auditory disabilities can occur in different hemispheres of the brain, causing a variety of problems. Knowing the details of an A.P.D. will make a world of difference to any child and family coping with it. When shared with a child's music teacher, the nature of the A.P.D. will suggest modifications to the teaching approach. Without this information, most music teachers are bound to become puzzled or frustrated as the student with an A.P.D. struggles to follow directions.

A visually oriented music teacher may hold the belief that reading music is the ultimate musical skill and focus on teaching your daughter to read music as a prerequisite to playing it.

It's critical that you seek out the right teacher for an auditorily challenged student. So many classical musicians are strong visual learners—a strong visual style is essential for playing complex classical pieces. But a visually oriented music teacher may hold the belief that reading music is the ultimate musical skill and focus on teaching your daughter to read music as a prerequisite to playing it. That places music theory at the beginning of the learning process rather than teaching it as an outgrowth of meaningful and creative musical activity. This approach does not serve children who need kinesthetic and auditory involvement early on, although it undoubtedly works well for those with very strong visual-spatial abilities. If your child needs auditory training and support, you are better off finding a teacher who enjoys working that way, right up front.

Pairing a primarily visual, remotely auditory student with an auditory teacher who concurrently teaches the visual components is likely to be this student's best match.

Your Spatial-Analytic Child

If your child naturally likes to view and analyze his physical environment in terms of size and measurements, distances and intervals, ratios and fractions, mass and force, he is a spatial-analytic thinker. To say that this child comes to enjoy numbers and understand what they express is an understatement. To him, they are essential tools for unlocking the mysteries of the universe. They are his tools of creation.

Learning to think and solve problems logically brings out special curiosity and creativity in the spatial-analytic child. He is the one who goes wild over erector sets, Legos, and K'nex. He wonders how big, how fast, how high or low, how unstoppable things are. He maps out schemes, small and grand. He is a natural-born scientist. Your spatial-analytic child may enjoy singing canons and playing musical arrangements that contain multiple melodic and harmonic parts because the elements overlap, synchronize, and work like a complex machine.

Spatial reasoning figures in significantly when a child is learning to understand music theory. The physics of sound, the order of scales and musical keys, and the structures of musical forms can all be regarded by a mathematical thinker as fun and interesting. A child with strong auditory ability accompanying such spatial intelligence may be able to follow an entire classical symphony and the changing movements within it. His special ways of thinking predispose him to succeeding as a traditional music student.

Making music is a full-sensory immersion—physical, auditory, kinesthetic, and totally experiential. So if your spatial-analytic child is not inclined toward kinesthetic or auditory learning styles, he may not begin to feel especially drawn to learning to make music in early childhood. The appeal of exploring music might occur to him later, say in upper elementary, middle, or high school. At that point, a music instructor could teach him the components of music using all kinds of spatial and visual exercises and activities.

The joy a young child derives from making music has little to do intellectual reasoning.

You can nurture the musical development of your spatial-analytic child by introducing him to recordings and performances of music anytime from birth forward. Try to include African, Asian, and Indian music in his listening experiences; these cultures create music in a wide variety of time signatures and scales that might tickle your child's logical mind.

When a spatial-analytic child matures enough to hear and discuss the structural elements of music and music theory, he will flourish in the hands of a visual-spatial teacher. Fortunately, this prevalent learning style is possessed by many music educators at all levels of instruction. Those instructors who've had extensive university training on piano, band instruments, or orchestral instruments are more than capable of working with your child. The best teachers will also include ear training, singing, composition, and improvisation in their teaching repertoire to provide every student with a well-rounded music education.

Your Auditory Child Who Is Not Spatial-Analytic

If your child is auditory but lacks the ability to understand, analyze, or remember spatial information, she faces a special musical challenge. She may be able to identify pitches by their unique qualities and to hear their placement in relation to one another. This makes it possible to sing and play music in tune. But grasping the placements of and the spatial relationships between written notes is another matter. If an auditory learner has trouble assimilating this visual-spatial information, reading music might feel as challenging as doing geometry. If the notes occur in ascending or descending order, the sequence could seem obvious to her. But when notes are found all over the staff, she might find that tracking and identifying them gets very confusing. Overcoming this hurdle requires lots of practice with manipulatives—teacher-speak for tangible representations of musical notes and symbols.

Children with spatial-analytic learning deficits or disabilities can improve their skills by working with a variety of exciting materials made of anything from plastic or cardboard to carpet remnants. Placing giant

Dance classes, water ballet, and martial arts boost directionality and teach children to navigate through space.

laminated notes on the lines and spaces of an oversized musical staff made of Velcro lines is one example of this kind of tactile, experiential strategy. Large motor activities and games can also help the auditory, spatially challenged child integrate spatial information through movement. Eurhythmy, a blend of music theory, movement, and dance included in Waldorf education may address this child's learning style particularly well.

If this description fits your child, you may also notice that she has difficulty reading maps, mapping diagrams, or following physical directions involving left and right. Directionality is one aspect of processing spatial information that trips up many of us! You'll want to find a music teacher who accepts your child's process and who has excellent ideas for improving her spatial awareness in music without neglecting other aspects of her training. A spatially challenged child can also benefit from participating in dance classes, water ballet, and martial arts. All of these boost directionality and teach children to navigate through space.

Your Grapho-Motoric Child

Like a visual child, your grapho-motoric child depends on written words and symbols to help him integrate new information. But more so than the visual child, the grapho-motoric learner should be the one who writes the words and symbols down. The act of moving ideas from one's mind into one's arm and hand and committing them to paper is the cognitive channel that works best for making new ideas stick. Once she has written things down, she can remember them. Writing works particularly well because it requires her to actively engage in two or three learning channels (auditory, visual, and kinesthetic) concurrently.

The grapho-motoric child may be a doodler, a copious diary writer, and a good correspondent. Regardless of the presence or absence of outstanding literary talent, she probably enjoys writing poetry and doing other kinds of creative writing to express herself. The process of thinking while writing provides the grapho-motoric person with valuable insights. When calculating math, she benefits from writing everything down in stages; skipping stages or doing mental math may not work as well for her.

When your grapho-motoric child studies music or anything else, encourage her to take notes so she will recall information later. It doesn't matter if she ever reads the notes again. The writing is what moves thoughts into her memory banks.

As a reinforcement activity at home, your grapho-motoric child can copy music from music books into her own notebook or music journal. In class, she'll benefit from copying down what she sees up on the board. Creating her own set of memory or flash cards helps her even more than reading or playing with them. But help her do both!

When your grapho-motoric child studies music or anything else, encourage her to take notes so she will recall information later. It doesn't matter if she ever reads the notes again.

Your grapho-motoric child will learn standard musical notation best by composing and writing music or copying music onto blank staff paper. She'll do well with a music teacher who allows time to make notes, assigns worksheets, and teaches music reading by getting her to compose a part, then write it down.

The grapho-motoric system works well in combination with other learning modalities. If a child is both grapho-motoric and visual, she'll get a lot from reading what she writes. If she's auditory, she may hear and hold onto the information she's writing down from a lecture or lesson. The reciprocal process of writing and listening will make learning music both pleasurable and memorable.

Your Kinesthetic and Tactile Child

Most children like to move around and touch things. The kinesthetic and tactile child learns best this way. In fact, staying in motion is this child's biological imperative. He swings his arms, bounces, skips, tumbles, and goes under and over things to learn about them. He runs his hands  over surfaces, rubs textured things against his cheeks, throws himself full tilt into crossing the monkey bars or eating an ice cream cone. He likes doing anything stimulating, at least for a little while until he needs to move again. This can include gymnastics, recreational sports, dance, performing arts, arts and crafts, cooking, hiking and biking, anything that involves sensation and action.

Perhaps you know a child or adult who paces or walks in circles during periods of intense thought. When the kinesthetic-tactile (K-T) learner moves, he concurrently stimulates his mind and begins to understand new information. Instead of distracting him, movement increases his ability to concentrate. He walks and thinks. The logic of this seems so contradictory that few teachers will permit a kinesthetic-tactile child to move during a period of focused learning. In a traditional classroom, K-T children try to conform, but after five minutes, they give up. Typically, an unpleasant dynamic between the child and teacher begins as the teacher tries and fails to keep the K-T child engaged in a lesson using strategies that work better for other kids. The end result can be disappointing for everyone.

When the kinesthetic-tactile (K-T) learner moves, he concurrently stimulates his mind and begins to understand new information.

The K-T style is more common than people think. In decades past, teachers frequently misinterpreted a K-T child's need to move as a sign disinterest or noncompliance. Now many teachers understand that the K-T child likes to learn as much as any other student. He just needs to move in order to do it. But the problem a K-T learner presents to a traditional teacher can seem monumental; she must encourage everyone else to sit still while making exceptions for the K-T child. A masterful teacher will find a graceful way to orchestrate such individualization, but such mastery is uncommon. Fortunately, music is one class that allows for both movement and idiosyncrasy.

If your child has a strong K-T style, you may already have run into casual comments from other adults about "hyperactivity." If your child experiences difficulty learning in conventional settings, you've probably heard the words "attention deficit." This can make a parent panic. Things can get particularly confusing when, in addition to having a strong K-T style, a child also suffers from a visual processing disorder or an auditory processing disorder. What teacher says or what teacher tells him to read may not make much sense to him. Those channels might be impaired. So naturally a K-T learner with a visual or auditory problem will begin to look for something else that can hold his attention. This can make him look very much like a child with attention deficit disorder with hyperactivity (A.D.H.D.).

It's critical to the well-being of this child that you make sure he is expertly evaluated. Sometimes even pediatricians need more specific training to be able to tell the difference between one set of symptoms and another. Best to take a very careful look with the help of an experienced, licensed diagnostician. A licensed resource specialist in the field of special education in combination with a licensed psychologist may be able to test your child to analyze exactly what is going on. Someone who understands a great deal about A.D.H.D. and processing disorders should also be involved. Some pediatricians are knowledgeable, but taking a team approach promises that your child will be considered from a variety of perspectives

Getting the correct diagnosis is essential for this child to receive appropriate treatment. The two paths of treatment could hardly be more different. A.D.H.D. is usually treated with medication, dietary changes, and/or biofeedback. The medications normally prescribed for kids with attention disorders may offer nothing to help a K-T learner with cognitive processing problems. Auditory and

The medications normally prescribed for kids with attention disorders may offer nothing to help a K-T learner with cognitive processing problems.

Your kinesthetic learner may have been born for marching band! visual processing disorders are treated with experiential therapies and the development of adaptive strategies for succeeding in school. If you can find ways to adjust your child's education to fit his learning styles and needs, you can turn things around before they escalate into problems. This kind of intervention will help your child have a positive school experience and a successful future. If things have already progressed beyond this point, you'll both begin feeling better when you get someone knowledgeable and experienced to assist you.

How does all of this impact musical development and music lessons? Good news! K-T learners are often natural musicians. They typically have strong physical intelligence that enables them to manage a musical instrument while they are moving. Your kinesthetic learner may have been born for marching band! Drum and bugle corps could be his greatest joy in high school. He needs music and action combined.

Music is a class where K-T children can experience joy. There, movement is often encouraged, even required, and multisensory learning abounds. The K-T learner can get his hands on xylophones, rhythm sticks, and an array of percussion instruments in the general music classroom. He can dance. He can move his body to demonstrate musical concepts. All this information may be visually reinforced, but the main tool for learning to make music is the human body.

What kind of music class will work best? You may wish to avoid a highly structured class in which your K-T child must stand at attention with a choral score or sit for 30 minutes at an electric keyboard. In the early months and years, classes such as Gymboree, Music Together, or My Gym introduce a K-T baby to music while he moves. Perfect match. In the early elementary years, dance and exercise classes might give the K-T child indirect exposure to music. Small group classes taught by teachers with training in Orff-Schulwerk, Kodály, and Dalcroze (see "Music Teachers and Programs") can provide K-T students with opportunities to move and use their senses.

Older K-T children will love and respond to music lessons that include dance, large motor games, and songs with hand and body motions. For children in the upper elementary grades, band and orchestra can be very good programs. There may not always be much large physical movement involved, but the children do use their upper bodies to play strings, brass, or woodwinds. There's never a dull moment when everyone is playing. The same thing goes for rock bands that get kids up on their feet slinging a guitar or moving in eight directions at once with a pair of drum sticks.

Spontaneity and individualization are luxuries granted most easily when children study music one on one.

Private music lessons can also work beautifully for the K-T learner; the creative private instructor is free to match his lesson plan and activities with your child's needs and responses that day. Spontaneity and individualization are luxuries granted most easily when children study music one on one. (Most teachers appreciate getting ideas from parents about effective strategies they can use for engaging children.) You may be most likely to find a K-T compatible music teacher offering instruction in rock, folk, or ethnic musical styles.

Any parent who suspects that his or her child actually has an attention deficit disorder should consider getting an accurate evaluation and diagnosis. If it turns out that a child has a true attention deficit disorder, I strongly recommend Thom Hartmann's easy-to-digest book *Attention Deficit Disorder: A Different Perception*, also known as the "Hunter in a Farmer's World" book. It sheds hopeful and refreshing light on the origins and benefits of A.D.D., providing parents with great insights for making the most of life with what has only recently become considered a disorder. Thom Hartmann presents a positive view of A.D.D. and A.D.H.D. His website (www.thomhartmann.com) offers free, ongoing mutual support for families and individuals living with attention deficit.

No matter what sort of style your child has, there's a chance it resembles yours. Why not take this opportunity to consider your own learning style? If you have some traits in common with your child, you may also have some insights and effective strategies to share with your child and his or her teachers. If your prevalent learning style differs from your child's, you may be able to develop new, mutually rewarding ways to communicate with each other.

Chapter 7

Learning Disabilities vs. Sensory Integration Disorders

What is the difference between a learning disability and a sensory integration disorder?

In the last chapter you read about learning styles and disabilities. You may wonder what specific learning disabilities are and how you can tell if your child has one. When we suspect we cannot reach or teach children through one of the basic learning modalities (visual, auditory, or kinesthetic), or when we notice that learning at school seems excessively frustrating to our children, it's time to take a deeper look. It's possible that a learning disability (LD) or a sensory integration disorder (SID) is causing the problem. LDs and SIDs are more common than many people would guess, and they definitely impact how kids acquire musical skills and abilities.

Children with learning disabilities have one or more cognitive modalities that are experiencing a delay, or are scrambled, underdeveloped, or impaired. Something goes wrong between your child's sensing of information and the incomprehension of it. Your child may see just fine but have trouble understanding what she has just seen. She may understand it but have trouble telling you about it. Somewhere in the brain, information has not been efficiently or effectively transmitted. Even so, your child is bright, capable, and creative. Her intelligence and the presence of a learning disability are two entirely separate issues.

If you suspect your child may have a learning disability, treatment is within reach.

With special intervention and assistance, many people are able to develop strengths and strategies that help them overcome most aspects of learning disorders. It's becoming common practice for people with LDs to seek educational therapy. Great strides have been made recently in the study and treatment of dyslexia, the most publicized learning disability. A specialist in educational therapy and treating dyslexia has tools to compensate for the disorder, even to overcome it. He offers any person with an LD specialized, effective coping strategies and compensatory approaches to learning.

An ED therapist is *not* the same thing as a tutor. Tutors help children complete their work. ED therapists teach children new ways to do the work themselves, creating solutions for children that last them a lifetime. If you suspect your child may have a learning disability, treatment is within reach.

Parents are entitled to request assistance and an individualized education plan (IEP) for their children. It is common practice for school psychologists and learning specialists to test children who've been experiencing academic or physical challenges in their classrooms. These tests often reveal the presence of specific challenges. Schools typically offer various types of therapy to serve all children with special needs. If you believe your child might benefit from an IEP, you can request one and follow through.

Sensory integration disorders are quite different than learning disabilities, but they also impact children's ability to function in musical and educational settings. Children with SIDs experience difficulty effectively integrating sensory information. For example, children with the SID called hypersensitivity often become overwhelmed and wound up from too much sensory input, such as loud noises, startling movements, and physical discomfort over the course of a school day. These children can bounce off the walls by dinner time in an effort to let it all out.

Children with the hyposensitivity are just the opposite. They seek stimulation because they don't pull in or compute sensory information as intensely or as often as normal children do. These children may seek noise, physical contact, and large motor activity in an attempt to satiate their desire to feel more. This can make them seem fearless or accident prone when their attempts to pull in more stimulation prove too dangerous.

In both cases, children with SIDs can appear to be easily distracted, physically wild, or overreactive to sensations and normal situations. Conversely, they can come across as unusually detached.

Having an SID can make a child's musical process unique. These children may need activities toned down or ratcheted up to meet their sensory input needs. A teacher who is sensitive to the child's energy level and reactivity to sound and environment can tailor a lesson to fit the child's needs. Done appropriately, learning to make music can be therapeutic for the child with an SID.

SIDs are most effectively treated by occupational therapy. If you think your child might be having trouble integrating sensory information, I encourage you to read *The Out-of-Sync Child*, by Carol Kranowitz. This handy paperback makes SIDs easier to identify and understand. Next, if your child seems to fit one of the SID profiles, schedule an evaluation with a pediatric occupational therapist (OT). If your child has an SID, the OT will teach you exciting ways to diminish the effects at home and school. Then your child will be ready to make the most out of studying music. All you'll need is a music teacher who is willing to integrate a few special sensory or calming activities into lessons in order to make music a positive part of your child's life. Feel free to ask your child's OT for suggestions.

When you choose a music program or instructor for a child with an LD or an SID, it's critical to fill in the teacher with the details of how your child learns best. Share strategic information.

When you choose a music program or instructor for a child with an LD or an SID, it's critical to fill in the teacher with the details of how your child learns best. Share sensory and strategic information. Develop an ongoing relationship with the music teacher, checking in briefly each week and asking for guidance about assisting your child with practice and enrichment activities at home.

If you advocate for your child at school by asking for individualized education, you can feel free to include the music teacher as part of your child's team of experts. This may prove beneficial to your child and to all the teachers as well. What a gift to your child to be considered by all the special caregivers in his or her life.

My eight-year-old daughter is kind of spacey. Her teacher says she doesn't pay attention at school. At home, she often forgets what she is supposed to do. School really isn't her thing, but I've been thinking that music might be. She loves to sing. She remembers whole songs from first grade. She puts on shows for the family sometimes, and she has asked us to get her singing lessons this summer. But with her poor listening skills, I wonder if it's worth the time, effort, and money. Do you think music lessons are going to go in one ear and out the other?

Not if you use a tape recorder!

Your daughter may actually listen well, but it seems she has trouble remembering what she just heard. This could be caused by environmental, psychological, or biological factors. She may need a different diet to boost her energy and attention. She could have an actual hearing problem. When was her hearing last checked? Unbeknownst to you, she may be coping with some kind of inner conflict that prevents her from concentrating on things going on around her. Or she could be forgetful as the result of a weak short-term, auditory, sequential memory. There are so many possibilities to check into, and so much to gain by doing so.

Your child's long-term auditory memory might be fine, as indicated by her ability to remember how to sing songs she has known for years. Perhaps a special strategy would help her move information from short-term into long-term memory. Children who need help remembering what they heard can learn to take notes and keep lists, or they can take the techie route and learn to operate a Palm Pilot-type device or a small tape recorder. This lets them record and organize information as it comes in. Writing notes works better for the grapho-motoric learner because it gets the old grapho-motoric channel involved. Techie approaches work better for auditory and K-T learners.

Since you have voiced a concern about your daughter's auditory forgetfulness, here are a few activities you can do at home to begin to assess whether or not your daughter might benefit from some new auditory learning strategies.

Children who need help remembering what they heard can learn to take notes and keep lists, or they can take the techie route and learn to operate a Palm Pilot-type device or a tape recorder.

- Plan a treasure hunt for fun at home. Hide five items in plain view throughout your home. Invite your daughter to play a game. Explain that you will soon tell her what the treasures are and she will hunt for them and bring them to you. You can offer a prize for each one she retrieves to reinforce every success. Before you name the items, explain that you will only repeat the list of items twice before she starts searching, and you cannot give her hints or reminders until the hunt is over. If she remembers the items in the list and can find four or more treasures, she is not having a problem with the task. Three finds raises a question about her auditory memory. Two finds or fewer suggests the presence of an auditory processing problem.

- Get your daughter's full attention, then verbally give her instructions to bring four items from her room. Ask her to show you the items in the order she hears you say them. See how successful she is. If she only remembers one or two items, or if she scrambles the order, have her auditory processing evaluated.

- Tell your daughter you want her to memorize the phone number of your nearest relative or close friend for safety. Tell her you will say the number once, then ask her to recite it back to you. Write down what she recites as she speaks. This way you can secretly look for errors. If she recalls only two or three of the digits and scrambles or invents the rest, this is also a sign that something may be amiss. Continue working with her on memorizing the number to complete the task. If she is unable to memorize the number after five minutes, just give it to her in writing to work on later. This gives her a way to accomplish the task gradually, and allows you to complete the assessment without making her feel inadequate.

If you believe your daughter is experiencing auditory trouble, it's wise to meet privately with her teacher to discuss the situation and develop some strategies for success. At this time, you can inquire about an IEP. Also, tell your child's pediatrician what's going on. Find out about getting her hearing checked. If the auditory problem isn't mechanical, you'll know that other testing is necessary.

If it turns out that your daughter has an auditory processing disorder (A.P.D.), then speech and language therapy or educational

Chapter 8

Singing in Tune and Perfect Pitch

Our daughter sings like a little songbird. We think she has the sweetest, most beautiful voice. She also sings pretty much in tune from what we can tell. But since my ear is tin and my wife's is probably chrome, we're not entirely sure. I've heard of children who were born with perfect pitch. How important is that?

Perfect pitch does not make a perfect musician, and a person with only relatively good pitch can accomplish great musicality. In other words, pitch and musical ability are separate issues, although having so-called perfect pitch makes playing in tune that much easier for musicians. So you are free to enjoy your daughter's lovely singing voice without worrying about her level of pitch perfection; even the rare one in 10,000 person who can pick a sound out of the air, name it, and sing it in tune still occasionally goofs up. What a relief for the majority of us!

What we refer to as perfect pitch is scientifically called *absolute pitch*, or AP for short. There are two kinds of absolute pitch. *Tone AP* refers to the ability to hear, identify, name, and sing individual notes in tune. *Piece AP* applies to remembering and producing the sound of the correct key of an entire piece of music.

Many children are born with an innate ability to hear and map pitches to some extent. But a small percentage of us are born with AP of one or both kinds. Science tells us that the level of maturity of one's inner ears as well as a genetic factor are at work. A study conducted by the Division of Biology

> *Perfect pitch does not make a perfect musician, and a person with only relatively good pitch can accomplish great musicality.*

and Human Genetics at North Shore University Hospital/New York University School of Medicine shows that 25 percent of musicians who tested positive for AP have siblings who also tested positive for AP. Scientists are working on mapping the gene for AP. So if you have more than one child and one possesses AP, the others may as well.

A child with AP is clearly in the minority, and you might consider this a somewhat rare gift. It's actually several smaller gifts wrapped up into one. And sometimes those gifts can feel to a child more like a nuisance than a privilege.

The ability to hear AP and to sing in tune depends on many discrete, interlocking functions. First off, your child's cochlea in the inner ear has to be healthy. (To find detailed information on the cochlea, please see "Resources.") Alfred Tomatis, the renowned French ear, nose, and throat specialist who created the Tomatis Method, cites the maturity of the cochlea as a key component to detecting sound frequencies across a wide spectrum. His method trains people's undeveloped cochleas to perceive sounds across an ever-broadening sound spectrum. Once the cochlea matures, he contended, a person is better able to perceive and categorize different pitches. His ideas are elaborate; many practitioners, musicians, and nonmusicians alike who've worked with his method report remarkable improvement.

Assuming a child's ears are normal and healthy, she should be able to perceive and discriminate between different sound frequencies, or pitches, in a general way. Then that child will be able to learn to categorize the sounds according to their relative distances to and from other known pitches. Next, she'll need to name them and store those named notes in long-term memory for future retrieval. Finally she will need to be able to retrieve those sounds from long-term memory when she hears them again or wants to sing. This means physical and cognitive processes must all be functioning very well in order for her to learn to sing relatively in tune. From the sound of it, your daughter is doing very nicely!

The good news for those 9,999 children out of 10,000 who don't inherit AP is that developing relative pitch (or RP, meaning "relatively good pitch") is simply a matter of ear training and practice. The more a child hears pitches, sings them, names them, and identifies them correctly, the better his sense of pitch will become. Playing fun ear-training games, singing in a choir, and taking instrumental or voice lessons during which students play or sing scales may all help in this regard.

Children who practice singing in tune and playing ear-training games before they turn six years of age have the best chance of developing excellent relative pitch. Kindergarten is the perfect time to get kids into music classes. Even pre-kindergarten is not too early for musical play with a purpose. If a child doesn't receive ear training early, he can still develop good pitch, but he'll probably have to work harder at it because the synapses in the human brain begin focusing only on known sounds at age six. At that age,

Berlioz, Wagner, Tchaikovsky, Ravel, and Stravinsky each wrote musical masterpieces without the benefit of absolute pitch.

higher-order thinking and conceptualization kick into gear as well, adding intellectual analysis to the way children evaluate their experiences. No longer are pitches heard as pure sound. They must compete with the child's thoughts about other things in the same moment, and they must be understood rather than being immediately accepted. So when parents hear some sour notes, they are well-advised to take a deep breath and smile because there's no point in feeling bad. The situation is far from hopeless, but ear training takes time. And patience. Lots of it.

You ask how important is perfect pitch? Some of the greatest composers of all time have been able to play music and compose successfully without having AP. Berlioz, Wagner, Tchaikovsky, Ravel, and Stravinsky each wrote musical masterpieces without the benefit of absolute pitch. So enjoy your little songbird and if she'll let you, sing along. Your tin and chrome ears could just polish up to a surprisingly tuneful shine!

My three-year-old sings to herself, but she sings nonsense words with a melody that strays all over the map. Her singing is kind of cute, but it doesn't sound very musical. I hesitate to say anything to her that might make her feel like she's doing something wrong. Should we even be teaching her to try to sing in tune at this stage?

Sounds like *you* possess a strong sense of pitch and musicality, and that you are really hoping your daughter will share those qualities. You are considerate to refrain from pushing or correcting your child's musical meanderings. Most three-year-olds do not yet clearly distinguish between pitches or sing them in tune. Few toddlers or preschoolers can sing anything recognizable. Singing approximate melodies is a sign of developmentally appropriate musical expression.

When do children become more melodic singers? Most do this as they acquire more fluent and expressive spoken language. The two functions occur in the same area of the brain, in fact. Children learn to modulate their voices when they speak, and concurrently, they begin imitating the melodic contour of favorite songs, mimicking the rise and fall of pitches. You might hear your daughter singing very high notes followed by some funny-sounding low notes. This is just her way of learning her way around a melody and exploring the possibilities. Eventually, this play should help her internalize the sounds of different melodic intervals. You can nurture her process by mirroring her sounds and playing along in the spirit of shared fun.

As for sing-song, nonsensical lyrics, young children who are just acquiring new vocabulary love to fool around with word sounds. They do this as a form of play and also to create new ways to express their thoughts and feelings. If your daughter's little songs sound vague and illogical, enjoy the silliness while it lasts. She's amusing herself. This is a sign of creativity!

Kids get more tuneful with time and experience, especially if you as a tuneful singer get involved. At four, children who are exposed to music and music education begin to sound more in tune and on time. Simple five-note songs are popular at this age. "Twinkle, Twinkle Little Star" and other children's songs with clear intervals such as *do* to *sol* fall perfectly within their auditory grasp.

We hope youngsters at five can match pitches do, mi, *and* sol. *By age six, they might be able to sing short songs independently in relatively good tune.*

We hope youngsters at five can match pitches *do, mi,* and *sol.* By age six, they might be able to sing short songs independently in relatively good tune. Beginning at this age, kids can develop the ability to conserve melodies: that is, recognize them without their lyrics or in keys and arrangements different from the original source. Every year brings greater refinement of basic skills along with the introduction of new ones. The whole process of musical development is exciting to witness and nurture.

Of course, all this development takes place more easily when children are exposed to music and have the opportunity to sing or play musical instruments. Even now, you can begin helping your three-year-old build her musical sensitivities and skills by listening to music and singing together, and by making music at home or in a parent-child music class.

If your child suffers or has suffered from repeated ear infections, learning to sing in tune may take extra training and time.

If your daughter is still sounding very out of tune by age five or six, you should consider getting her started with a music program that includes ear training. If you have more serious concerns, such as those that might arise if her speaking voice is monotonous or very raspy, you could consult a speech and language therapist. If your child suffers or has suffered from repeated ear infections, learning to sing in tune may take extra training and time. It's important to have her hearing checked and redouble your efforts to make her world more musically active. It is not unusual for children with chronic ear infections to have difficulty hearing and matching pitches. This can be helped through vocal training, educational therapy, or speech therapy with the right practitioner. Interestingly, some children who've had chronic ear infections during kindergarten and first grade also have difficulty learning to spell. This may occur because hearing is painful at the same time the child is trying to master the differences between subtle soft vowel sounds such as short *a* and short *e*. Again, we notice a link between language acquisition and melodic singing, since both occur in the same area of the brain! You'll probably begin to notice your funny songster singing in tune at about the same time she begins to speak to you in eloquent paragraphs.

I'm afraid I have an awful voice. I once jokingly compared it to a bullfrog and my teenage son told me not to insult amphibians. Just recently I went back to work teaching preschool, and I really want to have music time with my class. Of course, I worry my voice will set a bad example for the kids. Is my croaking potentially harmful to young ears, or can I go ahead and share music during circle time with my kids?

What if your students had music time with a teacher whose good pitch and lovely tone was overshadowed by a critical, perfectionistic attitude? Might that not do youngsters more harm than good? You are their teacher and you are the person they have a chance to sing with every day. Your students would rather hear your happy, out-of-tune notes than none at all! Besides, the more you sing, the better you'll get. And the truth is, few young children notice much about pitch anyway. Demonstrate your love of music, and that is what children will learn from you.

You can also expose your class to recordings of music played and sung in tune. Many teachers sing along with tapes in the classroom. This helps the hesitant singer find the right notes. Perhaps you'll even find some way to bring a musical friend, a music specialist, a retired musician, or a local musician to your class every so often to lead a music circle time.

As for your teenage son, most kids "shoosh" their singing parents and hurl clever little insults that make them feel extremely proud of themselves. Sooner or later they all give us the hook. Here's my advice: Never mind. Parents who ignore gnarly comments from their offspring are totally free to croon on. But if you truly feel unhappy with your own singing, maybe *you'd* like to experiment with singing a little differently.

Sometimes we sing songs in the wrong register. We think we ought to be singing high, for instance, so we squeak or screech when in fact our singing voices are naturally low. So try singing a familiar song in a different register than usual and see if you like the sound better. Do not ask your son for his opinion.

Some of us do not breathe enough when we sing. Our voices sound stressed and unsupported. We lose pitch and power, then our voices waver and crack. If this is your problem, you could work on breathing more deeply and allowing your exhalation to carry each note forward. This takes a fair amount of relaxing. If you want to give it a try, lie down on the floor, put your hand on your tummy and breathe in. Next, laugh with a big "ha, ha, ha." When you feel those *ha's* pushing your belly into your palm, you've found your diaphragm. No, not *that* diaphragm. See. You're laughing already. Breathing deeply enough to sing with support means you fill your body with air, then your diaphragm pushes it out when you sing a note or a line. The air gives you strength and better vocal control.

It's often true that where singing volume is concerned, less is more.

Some of us push our voices too hard. We nearly shout when we try to hit notes that feel too high. In this case, you could try singing more softly, approaching notes with an understated style. This makes a lighter, smoother sound. To get good at this, try singing in a whisper. You might be surprised by how pleasant and clear you'll sound. It's often true that where singing volume is concerned, less is more. You might also relax your jaw and open your mouth wider than usual to reach those high notes.

There are many other strategies we can use to improve our singing. So if these exercises sound fun to you, consider taking some voice lessons. It's never too late. Vocal training is a marvelously productive way to spend an hour every week doing something nice for yourself, and the little ones around the circle.

I've seen a course for improving pitch advertised in a magazine. I think you send away for cassettes. Could this kind of course actually help children learn to sing in tune?

Ear training that engages young singers in vocal exercises is definitely helpful, if they actually practice. But any cassette and book program is only effective if it matches your child's personality, musical range, and learning style. Even then, your child must be the rare soul who feels motivated to work independently. A cassette cannot respond to your child in any meaningful way. So on principle, I do not support pitch training with anything but a real human teacher. Your child could be slouching and singing out of tune through his nose, and the cassette or video lessons would have no way of noticing.

Receiving accurate, positive feedback about breath, tone, and note placement is essential for singers to develop better pitch and vocal technique. Without personal instruction from a teacher, a child doesn't know what to celebrate, what to change, or when to simply try again. Nothing beats a good live instructor! Of course, if none is available, you can attempt to make do with a cassette and book or video. Having a synthetic teacher may beat having none at all. I recommend video instruction from Homespun Tapes. Their teachers are personable, amusing, and talented. For contact information please check "Resources", page 225.

My six-year-old is plagued by perfect pitch. He cannot stand hearing the kids in his music class at elementary school sing out of tune. He says it sounds like "yowling" and he plugs his ears. This doesn't make him very popular with his peers. Also, he hates loud music and noises. How do we help him cope?

My tone-deaf grandmother might have said, "We should all be so lucky!" But as you know, there is a practical downside to having AP. In this world of recorded and live performances, out-of-tune notes can render young people with AP helpless. They cannot make the other kids sing in tune, and most kids do not sing in tune these days because they haven't been exposed to enough developmentally appropriate music. Schools haven't provided adequate music instruction ever since budgets for arts education were slashed.

The result is that we now have almost two generations of children who sing out of tune and laugh at their own singing voices. They gravitate to rap, a far less melodic form of music than popular styles of music from the 1980s and earlier. These days, a child with perfect pitch is surrounded by blaringly loud spoken or shouted words and hip-hop and rock rhythms. Their peers are other kids who may not listen to much melodic music and who do not, for the most part, have the chance to develop their musicality at school. They are part of a popular culture that feels alienated from classical music. (How often does the average child hear classical music these days?) This is a rough time for a child to have perfect pitch unless he has parents who actively introduce him to a wider variety of music and to other children who want to become musicians. Your son needs your support to honor his sensitivity despite social pressure to ignore or hide it.

First, I strongly recommend that you read about sensory integration disorders and look into the description of hypersensitivity. (See

"Resources" for further reading on SI disorders.) It's possible that your child is more sensitive than others in more ways than one. Occupational therapy has marvelous methods for reducing the intensity of some of these effects so children can function better in the real, noisy, and messy world.

You could also get your child earplugs or headphones so he can screen out unwelcome and overwhelming noises and sounds. Then, with sound protection in hand, you can take him to concerts and shows staged by professional musicians.

I'd also recommend talking up the good points of having absolute pitch. Kids with AP or good RP have an easier time making music. They generally have fun participating in special community musical projects and ensembles. If they sing or play and instrument well, they may join an honor choir or play with the city symphony even though they are younger than other players. They will never suffer the embarrassment of hearing a teacher tell them to "mouth the words." They will be more able to appreciate great music and great playing.

There's an added benefit. Kids with AP or good RP also have a distinct advantage when it comes to playing fretless stringed or other instruments that require an exceptional sense of pitch to find the desired notes. To play jazz and other microtonal music, musicians must possess a precise awareness of microtones, quartertones, and overtones. People without AP are far more challenged by intonation.

Finally, I hope you'll help your boy develop an excellent sense of humor so he can laugh at his desire for the impossible—a world in which everybody sings and plays in tune! Perhaps he can even find some compassion for less musical kids.

You can benefit your son and others like him if you take part in bringing music education back to schools. As a parent, you can lobby for music education with the school administration and your school's parent-teacher organization. If other children improve their pitch, your son's world will be that much more comfortable.

Rock-a-Bye Baby

When you tell a baby nursery rhymes, you can emphasize the internal rhythm by rocking her, clapping her hands together in yours, touching her tummy with your fingertips to the beat, or cycling her feet and legs in the air to the music. She'll like this as long as you  keep it gentle, and she may start to look forward to these rhythm activities as part of diaper changing, cuddling, and playing with you.

Celebrate! Celebrate! Dance to the Music!

You can help youngsters find the steady beat simply by crawling or walking to the sounds of music. Each even move forward represents a beat. If you are walking to the music, try adding one hand clap to each step, and you'll be walking and clapping to the steady beat. Feel free to add interest to this activity by changing the motions you  perform to emphasize the beats. A few popular moves include jumping up and down, tapping your head with both hands, flapping your arms à la the Funky Chicken, bending your knees, hopping like a frog or hopping on alternating feet, nodding your head, swaying your hips, and shaking your open hands up high and down low to the steady beat. Such open-ended movement helps youngsters discover the potential of their own bodies to feel and express music.

When everyone can keep the steady beat, it's fun to dance any way you like and still keep the beat going. Add the dynamics of volume and tempo changes, or invent dramatic characters doing silly or monster steps, and you can play this game again and again. For even more excitement, add the element of the quick "freeze" when you pause the music and see who can hold still. This one is a big winner at parties!

Simon Says, "Keep the Beat!"

A high-energy game of "Simon Says" to the beat, accompanied by a recording, can provide your family with lots of creative fun (and a good workout!). Parents or older children are most successful as the first leaders, and younger children may catch on as you go. When they feel sure of themselves, they'll ask for a turn to lead. Use body rhythms at all levels, reaching for the sky and stomping on the floor! Do not be afraid to bend, turn, or jump. Space is free for the taking, and anything goes.

Poetry in Motion

Reading for rhythm gives you a chance to accomplish two good things at the same time for your children. Reading aloud builds children's love and understanding of language. Reading rhythmic poetry and prose will help them develop rhythmic awareness, too. You probably already have a few of your own favorite rhythm-building books. Dr. Seuss is probably our most beloved rhythm-building author in this country, but others such as Jack Prelutsky and Shel Silverstein have written countless funny, rhythmic poems and stories that kids adore.

I Just Want to Bang on the Drum All Day!

The great variety of percussion instruments readily available from all around the world is enough to keep any kid or grown-up musically engaged. If you have a local music or percussion store, treat yourself to a family field trip and try as many as you can. I collect percussion instruments and also enjoy making them out of junk by fashioning them after the real things. Many books have been written on how to build your own percussion instruments, and several are listed in "Resources," including my own, co-authored with Ronny Susan Schiff, titled *Let's Make Music!*

Here are a few simple guidelines for exploring percussion instruments with your children.

- If you can find two identical instruments to play together, keep one and pass one to your child. This will allow you to mirror and validate your child's musical exploration and expression.

- Let your child explore the instrument first without giving her any examples or instruction. If you ask her an open-ended question such as, "How many different sounds do you think this thing can make?" you'll challenge her to use and trust her senses and musical impulses. She may also find her own unique approach to playing the instrument.

- Copy whatever sounds she produces on the instrument. This shows that you notice and like her discovery. Just as effective as mirroring your child's feelings, this musical mirroring helps her feel secure in her explorations.

- Create a mini rhythm jam by improvising a little rhythm pattern along with her pattern.

- See if either of you can find a different way to hold and play the instrument. Share your discoveries and jam again.

- Play the instruments together in many different ways: loudly, softly, quickly, slowly, and with a variety of short and long durations.

- Listen to what happens when you play different instruments and/or rhythm patterns together.

- After you've had fun playing around with instruments on your own, ask the sales clerk for a demonstration. The staff most likely knows traditional ways in which each instrument is played. It's always best to ask for education *after* you've engaged in some exploration and experimentation. When we think there's only one right way to play music, we eliminate possibilities by comparing everything else to the technique we've been shown by an expert.

- If you live in a town or vicinity without a music store that carries hand percussion, you can order basic kits or shop for any kind of percussion instrument imaginable over the Internet. Rhythm Fusion, Lark in the Morning, and Music for Little People are all excellent sources for percussion instruments and much more. Contact information is available on page 225 under "Resources."

- Once you own an instrument, spend enough time playing it to become proficient and comfortable. Then you can progress to the next stage: self-expression. When you are able to begin to take the mechanics of playing an instrument for granted, you'll be free to focus on developing musical ideas and expressing what and how you are feeling. At this point, the music we make can take on a life of its own. When we play, we feel better because we give voice to our inner world.

I'm with the Band!

Digging around in your junk drawers and cookware cabinets will provide every-thing you need to make a rhythm band at home. Yes, it will sound a bit comical, but the way you and your chil-dren get involved in playing on improvised instruments is what really matters.

Saucepans and big pots, right side up or overturned, make good drums. Scrub buckets and giant water jugs work well, too. Upside-down wooden bowls (especially on hardwood floors) make great clacking sounds. Pot and pan lids make great cymbals.

Mallets also make a difference in the sounds you'll get. Wooden tools such as wooden spoons, chopsticks, salad servers, and spatulas work very well. Metallic tools (not for the faint-of-heart) such as wire whisks, potato mashers, and slotted spoons can create a ringing, scraping, or donging effect on metal pots and bowls. You can even create a jazzy sound by moving the tip of a stiff paint or pastry brush in circles over the bottom of a large pot or bowl. You can use your home-made band to play along with music from any culture.

Deck the Hall with Spoons and Funnels!

Another fun trick is to string metal objects from around the house on pipe cleaners and suspend them from a dowel or broomstick balanced above the ground on a couple of chairs. You can sit beneath these items and play them with metal table-spoons for a delightful array of sounds! Hang odd-shaped kitchen utensils such as whisks, graters, and funnels to make interesting sounds. And, of course, you can play spoons by manipulating the handles of two metal or wooden spoons in one hand so that their bowls click together, as in the old-time style of playing bones.

When your instruments are assembled and placed within easy reach, follow the same steps for exploration and experimentation that are detailed above. Once you and your child are familiar with the potential of your instruments, it's only natural that you play along with a recording, or—best of all—as part of a jam with other musicians on a variety of instruments. Guitar, mandolin, piano, dulcimer, fiddle, and banjo, among others, make beautiful accompaniment for a rhythm band of any size.

You've Got to Move When the Spirit Says "Move!"

In a group of children, movement and rhythm go hand-in-hand or foot after foot. When we play music with a beat of any kind and ask kids to move to the sounds, all sorts of physical activities can become musical ones as well.

Young children do best if we give them complete instructions and verbal reminders such as calling out motions on the beat like, "Step, step, step, step." They also respond well to verbal challenges in time to the music such as, "Find a new part of your body to shake!" or "Switch feet!" When we introduce props such as balls, colorful scarves, batons, or hats, they can become even more creative with how they emphasize the beats. They can also play at being different characters that are moving in time to the music. This allows them to use imagination and body language dramatically, and it keeps their interest going. Adding new layers of interest to these rhythmic experiences will help you reinforce everything children are learning because they will be repeating the rhythmic actions while engaging creatively at other levels.

Children also love it when we speed up the music, and are equally relieved when we slow it down. This teaches them to listen closely to musical cues and makes them aware of how tempo influences our moods. You can blend all the activities listed above into a long rhythm and music session or try just one or two ideas at a time. It's all good.

To help kids calm down afterward, you can play softer, slower, and quieter music and have them move in smaller ways. Flexing fingertips, wiggling toes, scrunching noses, nodding heads, fluttering eye lids, breathing deeply—all these things will bring their energies down to make their next activity (and yours) go more smoothly.

I Can Sing a Rainbow!

Young children enjoy dancing with ribbons, swirling them, circling them, and waving them to the beat. You can select any recorded music with a strong beat, pass out the ribbons, join in, and create colorful shapes in time to the music.

If you've got a group of kids and a parachute, you can play parachute games that emphasize rhythm. When kids raise a parachute up and down together to the steady beat, they can count the time with their arm motions. When they move around with the parachute they can count the time with their steps. They'll enjoy running under and across the parachute, changing places, and much more. You can instruct them to walk to the left, walk to the right, make a wave by lifting and lowering the parachute one person at a time going around the circle clockwise, shake the parachute to the right and left in time to the music, walk under it for two steps and walk back out for two steps. You can find instructions for parachute games and activities on the Internet.

You Put Your Left Hand In

Teaching children to do simple line dances or folk dances in a circle helps them time their rhythmic movements to precisely match those of the other participants. This helps children develop their rhythmic coordination, listening skills, timing, and ability to follow directions. Why not start with what you know? The "Hokey Pokey" gets everyone into the action. Kimbo Educational sells a wide variety of folk dance and movement recordings that come with simple directions. Many include verbal directives on the tapes. For contact information, please see page 225.

Rhythm Sticks

Rhythm sticks are just two straight wooden sticks, also known as "lummi sticks," that children can tap together in a variety of positions to play rhythms. They can be purchased in music and toy stores or made out of dowels. They make different sounds when they are played on the floor, on a carpet, or on drums and buckets. Indestructible and inexpensive, they are an asset to any play group or preschool, and can be handy right on through the lower elementary grades. Kimbo Educational has three useful cassettes that will help a rhythm beginner get started. Check out "Lummi Sticks for Kids," "Simplified Rhythm Stick Activities," and "Multicultural Rhythm Stick Activities."

Too Cool for School

Bigger kids enjoy many of the activities detailed above, but they can also take advantage of the connection between playing sports and understanding rhythms. Of course, folk and popular dancing is good in the upper elementary years, but bouncing and dribbling balls, jumping rope, and practicing soccer skills can all be done to the beat of music. Sports such as baseball, kickball, basketball, and gymnastics all depend on players having a natural sense of rhythm and timing, so accompanying practice with recorded music from time to time can be an effective way of helping older kids make the musical-physical connection.

Chapter 10

Music and Intelligence

Lately I've been hearing people say that music makes people smarter. This certainly runs counter to what my parents told me when I told them I wanted to be a rock drummer when I grew up. Is there any truth to the slogan?

Everywhere we turn these days, we hear about research that proves how learning to make music helps children develop their intelligence. The data is so overwhelmingly positive that a school in Chicago recently began teaching all its academic classes with and through music. Even though some early research was flawed, more and more studies prove that learning to make music helps us build all sorts of new skills related to the perception, understanding, and creation of music. Not only do we develop musically; the same skills we gain through musical learning apply to other areas of thinking and doing. Students who've studied music score significantly higher on standardized tests such as the SAT. Ridiculous that funding for arts education is often the first item slashed when school budgets need reduction!

Dr. Howard Gardner, a forward-thinking professor of education at Harvard University, created his widely accepted theory of multiple intelligences in 1983. His ideas liberated people from evaluating intelligence based on a single concept and one IQ test score. He showed how each of us has many different capacities for knowing, solving problems and creating possibilities in our minds and worlds. We are all likely to be more intelligent in some ways than we are in others.

Making music has the potential to help our children utilize, develop, and strengthen several aspects of intelligence. Through studying an instrument, listening to music, and singing, they can tune up their minds and get excited about learning. This is likely to translate into getting better grades in subjects as diverse as language arts and mathematics.

How might music interface with some of Gardner's multiple intelligences? *Logical/mathematical intelligence* is the kind you see in kids who understand numerical patterns and mechanical logistics in the world around them. Their way of knowing seems automatic and effortless. These thinkers love figuring out the connections between things, analyzing the underlying components and elements in buildings, machines, and computers. You'll find such a child doing math for fun, making geometric origami shapes, and creating artful designs based on the patterns of interlocking shapes. This child has a strong spatial-analytic learning style, as is discussed earlier in this book.

Because music is inherently mathematical, the logical child will likely approach it as he would a puzzle or a riddle. Once he discovers the system or breaks the code, he will gain access to the secret knowledge! He might treat music like a medium with which he can build sonic structures and musical forms. He'll enjoy music theory, music software, MIDI processing, and recording gear. A child with less logical/mathematical intelligence will encounter a good mental workout when he tackles music theory, deconstructs a challenging piece of music into bite-sized passages, and explores the science of sound production. These exercises will benefit his mathematic and analytic abilities

Because music is inherently mathematical, the logical child will likely approach it as he would a puzzle. Once he discovers the system or the code, he will gain access to the secret knowledge!

A visually oriented child with good spatial-analytic skills will take to reading music like a fish to water. A child who intuitively hears and identifies the intervals between notes has exceptional auditory-spatial intelligence. The keys of a piano are spatially sequenced in a way that any child can see and feel. Stringed instruments present spatial possibilities that are both linear and complex. Learning to sing and make music of any kind provides children with unlimited amounts of practice using and developing their spatial intelligence through a constant experience of intervals and relative sounds.

Verbal/linguistic intelligence is obvious in children who express themselves eloquently through language, spoken and, when possible, written. Little folks who employ large vocabularies and excellent syntax are clearly gifted in verbal/linguistic intelligence. These kids are primed to become part of the oral tradition carried on by educators, poets, singers, storytellers, entertainers, comedians, and lyricists. Music students can improve their verbal/linguistic abilities and tools by learning and memorizing lyrics (building vocabulary), singing frequently (developing fluency), and composing songs (using expressive language). Songs help children learn to tell stories, express points of view, recite poetry, and turn language into exuberant syllabic play. These are all good ways to build verbal/linguistic intelligence and boost literacy.

Bodily/kinesthetic intelligence is evident in children with physical agility, balance, speed, and graceful coordination. Drummers need this kind of intelligence to coordinate their hands and feet as each one moves independently, interdependently, and simultaneously while they play the drum set. Rhythmically complex music demands bodily/kinesthetic intelligence from other instrumentalists, too. Coordinating fine and large muscle groups to pull bows, push slides, wield mallets, and depress valves in time and in tune will employ and improve any young musician's bodily/kinesthetic intelligence. Dancing and moving to music as part of music lessons provides even more of this experience. Playing a musical instrument can help anyone who feels klutzy become more graceful and can provide meaningful new ways for physically gifted children to excel.

Gardner postulated that the ability to hear and audiate music according to rhythms and melodic patterns, to hear pitch and play in tune, to play musical instruments, and to memorize and retrieve melodies and pieces of music merited its own separate category of intelligence. It is convenient to think of musicality as one cohesive form of intelligence. It certainly appears that way when we watch musical prodigies perform. They seem able to grasp the whole music-making process and take it beyond our wildest expectations. But, as you have read, I believe that musical intelligence amounts to a combination of many specific types of intelligence, expressed musically to varying degrees of success. Perhaps

Playing a musical instrument can help anyone who feels klutzy become more graceful and can provide meaningful new ways for physically gifted children to excel.

prodigies could be called *globally* gifted in musical intelligence, while the rest of us exhibit ability in just a few ways.

Even if we have an auditory deficit, experience difficulty with spatial reasoning, or are not particularly coordinated or visually oriented, we all possess enough potential to develop musicality and become good musicians. There is always room to grow, and always time to unlock and realize our musical possibilities. And if we help our kids get a good start, they will learn more easily, grow faster, and perhaps, by keeping things interesting, supportive and fun, they will stick with it and take it farther.

The back-to-basics approach to education wiped out school music programs in our town many years ago. Now our district wants to bring back elementary music education. It is planning to provide marginally sufficient funding for band and orchestra in grades four through six. Choral music ranks as third on the priority list, and music in the earlier grades has only nominal funding that could disappear next year. What should I say to our board of education to advocate for basic music classes with singing for the children in kindergarten through third grade?

Music is a basic part of any young child's day, and most classroom teachers depend on the expertise of a trained music specialist to provide quality instruction for their students. When there is no budget for a music teacher, music often disappears from school and along with it, most children's finest opportunity to develop basic musicality. When a district neglects primary-grade music education, children are unprepared to succeed in music programs in older grades. Primary music is essential.

Making music stimulates all kinds of abilities in young children during their most formative years. In particular, general music classes that feature singing and rhythm work combined with movement help primary-grade children develop musical awareness and abilities when their window of opportunity is open widest. The blend of music and language acquisition is also mutually beneficial to young children. To ignore the needs and potentials of these students when they are five, six, seven, and eight years old is, in fact, counterproductive to a healthy music program and it deprives children of essential early training. Your district must want children in grades four and up to succeed. So, of course, they need the basics of music to be introduced and taught well early on. This will help assure a sustainable music program and a high rate of student participation in music programs over the course of their upper grade years.

Also, if the schools only offer music classes to older children, the students in grades four and five will face the complex task of learning to play *and* care for an instrument at the same time they encounter pitch, rhythmic and composition basics. This means they will be asked to acquire all their musical skills at once. Pretty daunting. I call this a sorry round-trip ticket—into music and back out again. Much better to provide everyone with a fun and fundamental music education that includes singing, starting in kindergarten. This will prepare students to succeed when they enter a band or strings program.

Here are a few talking points to take to your school board if you want to promote general music education.

- Singing and learning to speak a language take place in the same part of our brains in the left hemisphere. Singing improves verbal and linguistic ability.

- Speaking and singing in English helps second-language learners acquire English.

- Singing promotes communication skills and self-confidence.

- Children who make music do better on standardized tests.

- Singing promotes students' physical and mental health. It relaxes them, gets them to breathe deeper and more frequently, feeds their brains with oxygen, and boosts their sense of well-being.

- Musical performances by students help build and sustain parent interest and participation in schools.

The multimodal nature of music education reaches every kind of learner. A musical school may be the happiest, healthiest kind.

If you are thinking about garnering support for music education in your school, it's easier to do if you are prepared with actual studies and

effectively, but certainly music therapists do, and most are sensitive, unconventional people who enjoy adapting activities to fit the specific needs of their clients. Music therapists are also trained to work as team members alongside psychiatrists, psychologists, doctors, and special educators in order to develop and manage individualized treatment plans that feature making music.

Some fascinating historical research suggests that music might actually impart cellular healing to the human body. Scientist Hans Jenny explored the connection between cellular structures and sound waves in 1936 with a famous series of experiments in which he placed tiny metal shavings on a tray above an oscillator. When he set the pitch frequency on the oscillator, the sound vibrated those filings and they jumped around on the tray, settling at the end of each specific pitch into beautiful patterns we often find in nature. Floral images, seashell shapes, patterns of droplets—these appeared in the filings when the oscillator stopped making its various noises.

Along related lines, the journal of the American Veterinary Medical Association and the Fauna Communications Research Institute recently presented research showing that the purring of cats functions as a "natural healing mechanism." Injured cats purr to help their organs and bones heal and grow stronger. Researchers attribute cats' ability to survive falls to their ability to instinctively produce healing sound frequencies. They say such vibrations can even improve human bone density, too.

Perhaps our bodies reorganize or heal themselves when they are vibrated by music. Maybe a diseased cell can actually revert to its formerly healthy structure or find a more harmonious one when massaged by a particular pitch. Maybe making music releases endorphins or helps our brains absorb critical hormones or serotonin, the natural brain chemical that prevents depression. There is still so much we can learn about music's role in health. Many studies are conducted through the International Foundation for Music Research out of the University of California at Irvine.

All the research in the world cannot supplant or validate the memories I have of children who have stretched beyond their so-called limits to sing, play an instrument, and dance with exuberance for all the world to see.

My grandchild has been labeled autistic. Can music therapy help him break through some of the behaviors that make it hard for other people to relate to him?

It's hard to generalize about how autistic children will respond to music and music education. Autism can manifest in a variety of ways, and children with the disorder are just as unique as those without it. For instance, children who have a particular form of autism called Asperger's Syndrome can be verbally expressive and intellectual. For these children, learning to make music may come naturally and be highly rewarding. But this profile could not possibly fit every child with Asperger's. Some need more quiet than others. Some need more structure. Others need less. Your grandchild could flourish with music lessons delivered in a manner suited to his specific needs and abilities. I hope you'll help him experience his musical potential with a creative and loving teacher.

Some autistic children have difficulty dealing with sensory overload. They may become overwhelmed by noise or intense music and might dislike the experience altogether. Some focus on particular sounds and repeat them to screen out other less attractive sounds. Some autistic children are fascinated, excited, or conversely calmed by music. The patterns, dynamics, and structures of music can appeal to logically minded autistic children. The repetitions in music may be soothing and pleasant to those who modulate their environments with auditory stimuli. Often, children with autism respond by moving to the music or joining in group musical activities that involve singing or playing instruments.

To understand what could be most appropriate for your special grandchild, perhaps you'll consider discussing the possibilities with his teachers, therapist, and a music therapist. (Many schools and centers for autistic children keep a credentialed music therapist on staff.) This is the most responsible approach to exploring what will work for him

It's very possible that when your grandson has established a positive approach to making music, he will be able to join a band or orchestra at school. Autistic children can be brilliant and enthusiastic musicians if they are given the support they need to thrive.

Chapter 12

Selecting a Musical Instrument

No one in our family considers himself a musician except Uncle Sam, who plays harmonica. We'd like our kids to get some music lessons, but we do not have a clue how to pick instruments for them. Where does a parent begin?

You've already begun your quest by posing this question. Many parents insist their children start with piano because they've accepted that as the common wisdom. It sounds like you are wide open to other possibilities, and someday your children will thank you.

Sometimes instrumental choices make sense, and sometimes they are purely intuitive on the part of a child. You know how some married couples resemble a pair of identical bookends but you wonder how others ever got together? The same is true for matching up kids with instruments. Sometimes the rules of compatibility make sense and a good fit is obvious. Sometimes you just have to scratch your head and enjoy the show.

Here are a few basic truths to follow when contemplating which instrument to study. One, everyone has to start somewhere but many of us don't end up with the same instrument we began playing in grade school. Your children need to find appropriate gateway instruments that will help them fall in love with making music while they acquire some general knowledge and basic skills. They can refine their choices as they get older and more sophisticated in

Everyone has to start somewhere but many of us don't end up on the same instrument we began playing in grade school.

their musical knowledge. Piano, flutophone or recorder, and guitar make excellent gateway instruments. Some school music programs include them. Children between the ages of five and eight who begin with one of these instruments can develop musical skills that will prepare them to play other, related instruments later.

Piano is the most linear and theoretically logical instrument of all. Its note range, size, and foot pedals endow it with an enormous range of dynamics. It's possible to express any mood and perform any style of music on piano. If you stick with it.

Piano physically prepares a child to play any keyboard instrument, drums, and some percussion. The striking, rhythmic action of the hands and coordination of hands and feet transfer well between those instruments.

Over the long haul, piano best suits the child with a hardy and sometimes contemplative personality and strong drive because it is large and potentially loud and requires players to sit up straight, moving fingers across the keys while positioning their arms and wrists above the keyboard. K-T learners and kids with strong physical intelligence might make good pianists. The strength, concentration, and agility needed to play complex pieces well is fabulous to witness but hard to accomplish.

As a gateway instrument, it is fine for almost every child, but not every child will or should stay with the piano. Between one and three years of study on piano may suffice before a child switches to something that fits her more specifically.

Flutophone and penny whistle recorder can help a child discover the beauty of melody while preparing to learn to play a larger, more demanding instrument. A child as young as four can begin to play flutophone or recorder, learning about breathing, mouth position, fingerings, and scales. School music programs traditionally introduce recorder during the third or fourth grade to teach children to read music and develop fine motor skills that could translate to a brass or woodwind instrument.

Some band directors suggest that children begin for a year or two with recorder, then progress to clarinet before learning to play, say, saxophone. This steps a child up from the lightest, least expensive instrument to the most substantial one with the greatest cost. In some regards, saxophone is easier to play than clarinet but it is heavier to hold and carry. Once a child can play clarinet well, saxophone comes much more easily, since the clarinet and saxophone are played similarly. This is why you see many professional musicians switch back and forth between the two when they work in a pop or jazz ensemble.

Guitar prepares children to play all kinds of stringed instruments, and for the primary-school student, it's a natural first choice. Classical guitar is the most challenging style; folk, rock, and country guitar are fun and relatively simple to learn. Of course guitar is exceptionally popular on television and radio, making it all the more attractive to many children. Guitars are light and portable. They are easy to rent, buy, and replace as children grow.

What physical ability does guitar require and promote? A child can play guitar standing up or sitting down. It does not require perfect posture, arm strength, physical power, or endurance, although these are useful qualities. Guitar allows children to sing while they strum the strings, and it gives them practice with basic rhythms and playing in time. Children who learn to play notes and scales develop the ability to move their fingers independently while pressing down firmly on the guitar strings. This gives them much-needed calluses that keep fingers from feeling sore. With guitar, children develop their musical ears and voices simultaneously, while learning to perform all sorts of wonderful songs.

Selecting a musical instrument for your child can be almost as logical as solving an algebraic equation. The more you consider each instrument's value and each child's variables, the nearer you'll get to finding a solution. Apply some intuition as well and you'll arrive at a decision that reflects your child's musical tastes, personality, and physical abilities.

There's just one hitch. When a kid gets excited about playing a particular instrument, you may find yourself talking sense till you are blue in the face. His drive to learn that instrument may override your brilliant logic and could point you both toward the best choice against all odds. Under those circumstances, it's best to summon your dedication and help that moonstruck kid tackle whatever obstacles arise in pursuit of his artistic vision. Parenting is just like that sometimes, isn't it?

One thing is for certain. No matter what instrument they choose to play, if you take a proactive role in helping your children decide, you'll spare them from being randomly assigned instruments by the school band or orchestra director whose need may be finding somebody to play bassoon. There's nothing at all wrong with bassoon if it fits a person's taste and ability. But it's not everyone's cup of tea. Garrison Keillor of *A Prairie Home Companion* radio show fame once suggested that the only time most of us ever get to hear a bassoon is on Saturday morning cartoons when some large character lumbers or galumphs across the screen and falls off a cliff. Think about it. Your kid should love that sound to play that instrument.

In the name of making good instrumental choices with your children, here are a few no-nonsense pointers:

- Consider your child's size and physical strengths. Is she robust and energetic, capable of expressing and channeling big energy through a physically demanding instrument? Cello and string bass require strength and power, as do drums. Violin requires strength and endurance. Trumpet takes arm power. Guitar conforms naturally to the body in repose. Think about what each instrument asks of the musician.

- How long or short are her fingers? Long fingers are perfect for reaching across piano keys and strings. Short fingers can do just as well, but the musician has to work a little faster or stretch a little farther.

- How is her sense of pitch? If it's accurate, she'll do well on a fretless stringed instrument such as violin or any other instrument where the notes are not clearly defined by visual or physical markers. If not, she'll need an instrument that has absolute positions for hitting all the pitches accurately. Fretted stringed instruments (such as guitar, banjo, and mandolin) and piano are good examples.

- Is she is a rhythm ace? If so, she could be pleasantly challenged by learning to play drums or percussion of any kind, or instruments that can be played percussively such as piano, bass, or guitar. She would also be able to apply that rhythmic ability to lead instruments in jazz such as saxophone or vibes.

- Is she all lips? Does she blow on bottles and imitate a bugle for fun? Can she fill a balloon faster than you can? Maybe a mouthpiece or reed would be the natural top end of an instrument for this child. Think brass and woodwinds or pipes.

- How would you describe her musical tastes? Of course, they will probably change over time, but if she already has strong preferences now, it's wise to take them into account. If she adores country, folk, or bluegrass music, then guitar, banjo, mandolin, or fiddle might make good first instruments.

If she is an expressive person, sensitive and soulful, your child might enjoy playing piano, violin, clarinet, saxophone, or another instrument whose voice is known to convey powerful emotion in symphonic music.

- How does your child's personality match up with different instrumental voices? If she is an expressive person, sensitive and soulful, your child might enjoy playing piano, violin, cello, clarinet, saxophone, or another instrument whose voice is known to convey powerful emotion in the context of symphonic music. If she has a milder nature and is drawn to gentle sounds, she might relate more to instruments with a light, introspective, or calm quality such as flute, guitar, harp, viola, French horn, or oboe. A humorous, energetic child might enjoy brass or woodwind family instruments for their boisterous and whimsical characteristics. The highly kinesthetic child might enjoy playing rock 'n' roll drums or percussion.

- Is your child a natural singer? If so, then piano or guitar lessons could help her learn to accompany herself while she concurrently develops two sets of musical skills, and studies voice.

If you arrange to take a family field trip to a music store that carries all kinds of musical instruments, your child will be able to get a sense of how it feels to hold various instruments. A picture is worth a thousand words, and real, hands-on experience is worth a million.

My husband and I have been having a family feud for weeks about which instrument our daughter ought to study. She wants flute lessons, and that sounds just fine to me. But my husband favors violin, and he's been pressuring her to take violin lessons against her wishes. Is there some way you can help us to settle this matter?

Choosing a musical instrument for your child has obviously become a complicated process for your family. Many families experience the same thing when there are two competing ideas and one child. Let's see if we can lay out a course of decision making so you can reestablish some harmony at home.

Sounds like your husband is determined to get his wish. A loving father wants his child to accomplish more than he did, even if she doesn't want to. A very wise father comes to terms with the difference between his wishes and what will best serve the child.

Bottom line, your daughter needs to choose an instrument that will be right for her, and it might be flute or violin. Or it could be bagpipes! How do you figure this out?

You might find a way to unlock the situation if you can take a step back. Your husband is being persistent about violin lessons for a reason and is presently unwilling to open up to other ideas. Perhaps the key to his persistence is buried in personal history. Can you begin a compassionate discussion with your husband about his childhood musical dreams and experiences? See if he'll talk to you about what he did or did not achieve. Healing that wound could free him up to study violin now as an

> *A loving father wants his child to accomplish more than he did, even if she doesn't want to. A very wise father comes to terms with the difference between his wishes and what will best serve the child.*

adult. Maybe your daughter will surprise you both and ask to study with him.

Is it possible that your husband loves the sound of violin or holds it in particularly high regard because of something he learned in the past? Ask him to tell you about the origins of his passion for violin. He'll probably share at least one story you've never heard before.

You might also appeal to your husband's logical side. Violinists need upper body strength and excellent posture to hold a flute or violin and bow. A child with low physical stamina may burn out on violin and could be better off playing an instrument that is less physically demanding. It would be practical to engage him in a discussion about your daughter's physical strengths, learning styles, and musical tendencies.

Violinists must possess a strong sense of pitch to be able to play in tune. As is the case with all nonfretted stringed instruments, every note is found by ear and by hand. How is your daughter's pitch perception? Flute requires discipline and patience for developing tone. Does your daughter possess a determined, patient personality?

Do you know how your daughter feels about the violin and flute's usual roles as lead melodic instruments in various styles of music? Enjoying the sounds of music played by a particular instrument should be a prerequisite for a serious course of study on that instrument. For now, there is much to be gained by exploring many musical styles to see if she leans more in one musical direction than another. This could point you toward a particular kind of instruction.

After a thorough exploration of your daughter's compatibility with violin and flute, you should have a clearer idea about what instrument she may enjoy playing more. The next goal is to begin study on a trial basis. Many music stores rent student instruments by the month, and some have rent-to-own programs that allow you to buy an instrument after paying rent toward the purchase price for a few months. At the three-month mark, you can check in and decide whether to continue or switch to a different instrument. You know the old saying, "Seeing is believing"? Sometimes it takes a few attempts to see how your choices are shaping up.

Logic and careful consideration aside, perhaps you simply feel that your husband is

Enjoying the sounds of music played by a particular instrument should be a prerequisite for a serious course of study on that instrument.

too pushy and that your daughter really needs and deserves validation to do as *she* pleases. Then you may just have to resort to something women have always done when trying to change their husbands' minds. However, I am not at liberty to discuss *that* in this book.

My eight-year-old has very weak fine motor skills and not much upper body strength, but he really enjoys singing. Could voice lessons be a reasonable introduction to music education for him?

Why not? Voice instruction is usually a central part of any general school music class, so most people do not think private vocal instruction is necessary for grade schoolers. But there is a lot to learn about the voice and it provides an excellent vehicle for learning all about music and music theory. You just need the right teacher.

Voice lessons should teach your child to use his voice properly, creatively, and powerfully. He'll learn how to take care of his vocal chords. A versatile teacher can help him learn both classical and popular vocal techniques, and experiment with different musical stylings. Voice lessons would also give your son general musical skills and theoretical knowledge if it includes reading and writing music. In time, voice lessons could help your child develop a sense of his own sound. With a good singing voice, your son may decide he wants to be a lead singer in a garage band, join a children's choir, or perform in the musical theater. Right now, he doesn't need to know how popular it might make him with the girls right around sixth grade.

Health tip: private voice lessons can help children who have raspy voices avoid further vocal complications. They may be straining their speaking voices every day. These children can benefit from early intervention that will prevent them from scarring their vocal chords later in life as a result of developing nodules or nodes. That condition may require surgery and an extended period of recovery.

You might also consider percussion or drums for your son. These require more large motor coordination and help kids build endurance without taxing their ability to lift very much.

My seven-year-old is just wild about guitar. He wants to play electric but I don't think my wife and I are ready for that just yet. We're going to start him off on an acoustic instrument and let him beg for an amp until he's about ten. Then we'll see. How do I know what size of guitar to get for him?

Did you know that children can practice electric guitar with small, quiet amplifiers or using headphones? You can even find children's-sized electric guitars these days. Solutions are only as far as the nearest music store So let's discuss how to choose the right-sized guitar, electric or acoustic.

Guitars for young children can be purchased in one-quarter, half, and three-quarter sizes. Bigger kids might be ready for a full-size guitar by the time they complete middle school. Like everything else, it all depends on your kid. Sizing a guitar is something like the story of "The Three Bears." We want the one that's "just right." Here are some rules of thumb:

- Relative sizes of guitars vary from maker to maker. One guitar manufacturer's idea of a half- or three-quarter-sized instrument can be very different from another's, so your child should try each one at a music store to see what fits best.

- In general, children in preschool through kindergarten are most comfortable with half-sized guitars, which are not much bigger than ukuleles. Kids who are tall for their age might be ready for a three-quarter-size guitar as early as kindergarten, but this is unusual.

- Few quarter-sized guitars stay in tune or sound good. The most playable ones cost quite a bit because the work involved in making a quarter size is the same as it is for a larger guitar. If a child is too small for the half-sized instrument, you might consider starting with ukulele. Ukes make  very friendly first instruments—or second or third instruments!

- From ages four to six, your child may fall between sizes for guitars. Torso size, arm length, and the specific measurements of various brands of small guitars must be carefully matched in a guitar that fits well. Some people buy one that's a little large and place a capo at the fifth fret to reduce the distance the child's arm has to stretch to play notes or chords. But this only works if the body size is small enough that the child can reach over with the other arm.

- Usually, beginning at around age seven, children can get their strumming arms over the lower bout of a three-quarter-size guitar.

- Regardless of what size guitar you rent or buy, it's in your best interest to make arrangements to exchange it or trade it in when your child is ready for the next larger size.

The country singers we watch on TNN all have steel-string guitars. I love that sound. But the fellow at the music store suggested we get our daughter a nylon-string guitar instead. Does this mean she needs to learn to play classical music?

Choosing a steel-string guitar or a nylon-string guitar for your child's first instrument should reflect your child's hand strength and her ability to tolerate temporary discomfort. That first guitar should be one she can play comfortably. Nylon strings are easier on the fingers for children who are more sensitive to pain. Once your child has calluses and basic guitar skills, you can refine your choice of instrument and musical style. For this reason, many parents decide to rent first guitars for their children. Those who purchase instruments should keep in mind the possibility that they

will want to trade up or sell that first guitar to get one more suitable in a year or two.

The kind of guitar you select need not determine the style of music your child will learn to play. The only style that truly mandates use of a nylon-string guitar is classical music. Yet these days we are treated to the music of classically trained guitarists, such as William

Coulter, who perform on steel-string instruments when they adventure into the broad terrain of fingerstyle and Celtic music. Rock and country usually feature steel-string guitar. But Fleetwood Mac guitar legend Lindsey Buckingham frequently puts an acoustic-electric nylon-string guitar in the lead. These days, people blend styles and cross over from one sort of guitar to another to pioneer a variety of marvelous sounds. Your choice of guitar and style can be a very personal one. Respect tradition or blaze a new trail; it's up to you and your child.

How do you determine what will work best for your child? If she can withstand some discomfort in the beginning, steel strings could be a reasonable choice as long as the action (the distance from the strings to the fingerboard) is made low (i.e., easy) enough. If your child is more pain sensitive, softer nylon strings will be easier for her to strum and press down until she develops greater hand strength and calluses. Many children begin on nylon-string guitars.

Very few children begin playing electric guitars. The technology adds an extra component to a child's early learning process, and the amplification gives your child the opportunity to crank up the volume and rock out. From a physical point of view, playing electric can feel challenging to some youngsters. Many electric guitars are solid wood and heavy. The rugged, hardy kids can probably "sling an axe," but you might want to consider the ergonomics of your child's developing spine before you choose anything too weighty. Sticking with an acoustic guitar until children can confidently play chords and scales, strum, and sing works well. The prospect of getting that electric guitar later makes good incentive for practice, too. Again, if our child has her heart set on an electric guitar, you might just work out the details and help her satisfy her curiosity.

As you have undoubtedly discovered, children can make pretty tough customers. That's one good reason to shop for guitars where you can try them out and listen to as many as you like. This also allows you to check for size and ask the sales staff for a good deal or family-friendly payment arrangement.

If you are planning to hand your child a guitar from under the bed or up in the attic, it's helpful to check the size and find out what kind of strings the guitar is meant to hold.

If you are planning to hand your child a guitar from under the bed or up in the attic, it's helpful to check the size and find out what kind of strings the guitar is meant to hold.

Old guitars need new strings. Please remember that nylon strings are not interchangeable with steel strings. Guitars meant for steel strings are built to handle higher string tension than guitars intended for nylon strings. If you restring a steel-string guitar with nylon strings, it's likely that the nylon strings will be too slack; they will go out of tune easily and buzz. Definitely do *not* restring a classical guitar with steel strings. The bridge will probably pop right off!

If you are planning to offer your child a guitar from "storage," it's best to ask an expert for help. Someone at a local guitar shop should be able to identify your instrument, make any necessary repairs or adjustments, and put a fresh set of strings on for you. Feel free to ask the guitar tech for a free lesson on restringing your guitar at home. When that first string breaks, you'll be able to overcome panic in a flash and save the day so your child can keep on strumming.

Chapter 13

Choosing a Music Teacher and Program

There are a bunch of different music programs around our town. Some of our friends have kids studying Suzuki violin. One's child goes to Kindermusik. The next door neighbor swears by Music for Young Children. How should I go about finding the right music program for my daughter?

Choosing the best music education program for your child means playing detective: gathering information, interviewing teachers, and visiting classrooms. To find one that's right takes more than flipping through the yellow pages.

Let's start by learning a few basics about prevalent music programs. In the pages that follow, you will find descriptions of a handful of influential methods for teaching music to young children as well as several prominent music education programs widely available in the United States. The "Resources" section at the back of the book lists contact information for these programs in case you want to request more information. Not included in "Resources" are the regional and local music programs unique to your area that combine music, movement, and other arts into homegrown curricula. To find out about what your town has to offer, you can contact your local chamber of commerce and start making phone calls. Best to leave yourself several weeks to make inquiries so you can make a calm and careful decision. It's important to get any child into a program or lessons with a teacher that matches his abilities, needs, and preferences. As we've discussed, a good match is the ticket to success.

Dalcroze Eurhythmy

Swiss pianist and composer Emile Jacques-Dalcroze (1865–1950) designed a series of exercises (movements) and classes called *eurhythmy*, incorporating dance with music. You will find his system for singing and sight-reading at the heart of many music education programs, even those that do not bear his name. All children—espe-

Waldorf schools incorporate Dalcroze eurhythmy in their programs.

cially kinesthetic learners—can learn a lot about making and reading music with his techniques. Waldorf schools incorporate Dalcroze eurhythmy in their programs. Any music educator can train in Dalcroze techniques, so while there is no Dalcroze school, any instructor you interview might have experience with the methods. It's good to ask

Kindermusik

Kindermusik classes provide music education to children between ages birth and seven. As a family-oriented program, Kindermusik asks parents to take an active role in their children's musical development by giving them supplemental activities to do at home each week. Classes are usually small and personal, and they are often held in community meeting places. The program supplies specialized learning materials.

Kindermusik teachers integrate prevalent music education techniques to teach children to perform, read, and compose music in an ensemble fashion. The classes get children singing and playing many different musical instruments, including those from the Orff Schulwerk tradition (see page 136). Kindermusik teachers study child development and learning theory in addition to music education. Classes are lively, fun, expressive, and filled with traditional music.

Kodály

Kodály training has helped music educators develop what most parents think of as a good general music education in school. Hungarian maestro Zoltán Kodály created a formula for well-rounded and successful musical development based on singing first and instrumental music second. He said, "The human voice is the only instrument which is available for everyone. Our age of mechanization leads along a road ending with man himself as a machine; only the spirit of singing can save us from this fate." His concept includes singing folksongs from many nations; music reading and writing (musical literacy) and solmization (singing the name of the tone to learn pitch and value); and choral music, including Kodály's compositions of two- and three-part singing exercises for all levels of music education. Teachers trained in the Kodály method help students develop these qualities concurrently: a well-trained ear, a well-trained intelligence, a well-trained heart, and a well-trained hand. Kodály influenced training helps students become successful choral singers.

Music Learning Theory and the Gordon Institute

Music educators who wish to develop their individual teaching strategies and curricula can receive specialized training in Music Learning Theory (MLT). This takes into account child psychology, learning theory, and developmental factors that affect how children learn to make music. At the heart of MLT is *audiation*, Dr. Edwin Gordon's expression for imagining and understanding music within one's mind without having the actual physical experience of hearing it. Dr. Gordon has written several books with CDs in a marvelous series called *Jump Right In* that present MLT music education curricula for children of all ages that are utilized by music educators everywhere.

Music Together

Music Together classes are playful parent/child music and movement groups for kids up to age four and their parents. Each class includes a great deal of creative movement, singing along with the teacher, playing, keeping time, dancing along with the teacher and special Music Together recordings, and participating in rhythmic jam sessions. All this gives young children the message that they can make music, invent music, and express themselves musically and physically.

Music Together teachers are an eclectic group of musicians, child development specialists, and therapists, all trained to run their classes by Kenneth Guilmartin, founder of Music Together, and his colleagues. Each teacher brings a unique personality and style of musicality to the class, so look for the right match for your child. Specialized materials are provided for making "Music Together" at home.

Music for Young Children

Music for Young Children offers a balanced and comprehensive keyboard-based program for children between the ages of three and 11. This multimodal approach to teaching music fits every kind of learner. Kids dance, sing, play keyboards, play percussion instruments, compose, share their creations, and play lots of great games that help them learn to read and write music notation. Exciting teaching methods and activities keep the classes moving right along through every basic component of music education, with instruction in keyboard, singing, solfège, rhythm, ear training, sight-reading, theory, history, and composing, all rolled into a single lesson each week. Small classes allow kids to be seen, heard, and acknowledged. Classes are highly structured and fast paced.

Music for Young Children also offers Sunrise, a starter program for two- and three-year-olds. Small groups of preschoolers meet in the teacher's studio, or in a nursery or day-care setting, for 45 minutes every week. Through singing, rhythm, and listening activities the children are introduced to the exciting world of music. The group encourages listening awareness, development of fine motor skills, and social interaction and helps develop attention span and confidence.

Orff Schulwerk

Orff Schulwerk is a child-centered approach and music education methodology developed by Carl Orff and his associate Gunild Keetman that teaches children to make music based on doing things they enjoy. Students sing, chant rhymes, clap, dance, and keep a beat on anything nearby, including their heads, shoulders, knees, and toes! These activities combined with a sprit of open-ended discovery free the imagination and get students hearing and making music first, then reading and writing it later. This is the same order in which we acquire language skills. When the children want to remember their own compositions, they begin learning to write and read music. Although this sequence of instruction works well for all learners, it's particularly beneficial for grapho-motoric and auditory children.

The special Orff melody instruments are very exciting, welcoming to children, and beautiful to hear. They include wooden xylophones and metal glockenspiels of varying shapes, sizes, and pitch ranges. They can be adapted to the level of ability of any player, so children can improvise and play parts well at their own levels of competence. When students play the instruments together in a small orchestra, they learn to be sensitive listeners and cooperative participants. This hands-on approach gives kinesthetic children a comfortable channel for their energies, and it gives visual children a lot of practice using their hearing and creativity to become good ensemble players.

As with Dalcroze, there is no Orff Music School. But there are more than 10,000 teachers in the United States who offer Orff Schulwerk as part of their music education classes. Anyone can train in the method, and many music teachers with degrees have had at least some exposure to the approach.

The Suzuki Method

Founded by Dr. Shinichi Suzuki, the famous Suzuki teaching methods involve extensive family participation with one parent learning the instrument right alongside the child. Parents and kids practice together; the adult becomes a role model and an ongoing source of motivation for the child throughout the education process.

Suzuki instruction features a structured program, excellent for parents and children who flourish in an orderly environment with clear-cut goals. Students acquire musical skills as they become ready by following a prescribed educational path. This assures that children receive a well-rounded, thorough music education.

Infants get an early start with the Suzuki method by listening to the recommended music and internalizing the melodies. By age three, they have already committed the Suzuki repertoire to memory, and are ready to learn to play the pieces by ear. This approach is particularly effective for prereaders as it relies upon and develops auditory listening skills. Visual children might benefit from this method because it gives them a lot of practice using their ears and auditory memory.

Suzuki teachers attend workshops together, sharing information and assisting each other by coaching one another's students during week-long workshops. This collective approach gives students a chance to reap the wisdom of more than one teacher while sticking with the same method.

Suzuki violin lessons are among the best known and most popular lessons, but Suzuki guitar lessons are also available in some areas.

Yamaha Music Instruction

Yamaha music schools have sprung up in a number of communities in recent years. The music instructors work in keyboard studios where synthesizers are hooked up to computers and can be played using the Yamaha Music Education System. The approach endeavors to help children become well-rounded musicians through a series of structured courses, each one ending with an assessment. This style of music education is fine for children who can go with the Yamaha plan, but might be unnecessarily challenging for those with special needs or deficits in certain styles for learning. The assessments, which are intended to keep every child on track, assume that all the students in the class are able to keep up with the program. The computer element may prove motivational for children who typically have trouble staying focused, and for those who like to learn at their own pace.

In general, the curriculum takes into account the physical, intellectual, psychological, and social needs of the students, presenting them with new challenges in a developmental sequence. Children can begin as young as three years old. When they are four or five, they can enroll in the Junior Music Course and stay with it through six years of classes that emphasize ear training and rhythmic development, keyboard playing, singing, solfège, playing in ensembles, and, of course, musical games. Parent participation, especially at home between lessons, is essential to Yamaha programs.

The computer element may prove motivational for children who typically have trouble staying focused, and for those who like to learn at their own pace.

Yamaha is primarily known for keyboard-based music instruction but has grown to include (in some locations) guitar, voice, and flute instruction as well. Yamaha has also developed computer software for small-group keyboard instruction and keyboard labs in academic schools. To learn more, you can surf the Web and read all about the programs in detail.

My lack of musical experience makes me doubt my own ability to find the right music teacher for my child. Can you please recommend some ways that a parent can sift through the possibilities to find that special person?

Parents face a complex task in evaluating a potential music teacher. That's probably why you're feeling unsure about the process. It helps to have some specific questions to ask, and guidelines to follow as you consider the character of the teacher's answers. Even those of us with a lot of musical experience can feel challenged by the process of evaluating music teachers and programs. There are so many variables to consider.

Choosing an effective music teacher is a bit like selecting a personal physician. The diplomas on the wall and that shiny brochure are important, but all too often, they prove to be nothing more than pieces of paper filled with carefully considered words. The real proof of a teacher's gift is in the process. A teacher may use a methodology founded upon a stellar developmental philosophy. A teacher may hold a master's degree in music from an Ivy League school or a fine music conservatory. But a great teacher needs much more than training to turn making music into a magical experience for her students. She needs heart, spirit, and dedication.

Your gut reaction to any teacher is important to notice and respect. Because making music is such a personal process, you and your child need to know that you will receive personal care. Teachers with good interpersonal skills, common sense, and emotional sensitivity can turn even limited musical training into a gateway to musical development for children.

As children mature, some will become serious music students who can tolerate the demands of "tough love" teachers whose techniques help them get outstanding musical results. But all musical beginners need TLC as part of the package.

Before you choose a teacher, put together a list of candidates and start collecting information about them. You'll want to know their background as musicians as well as what music education training they've completed and any special certifications they've earned.

> *Teachers with good interpersonal skills, common sense, and emotional sensitivity can turn even limited musical training into a gateway to musical development for children.*

A master's of arts degree in music or music education tells you the teacher possesses a strong foundation in music theory and performance. It gives you some assurance that the teacher takes her work seriously and has proven her musical ability to experts in the field.

Earning an advanced degree is only one way music teachers develop professional expertise. Some music teachers have pieced together their training without ever going to college. If a teacher has participated in private training seminars based in a specific methodology, you're probably in capable hands. Certification in the techniques of Orff Schulwerk, Kodály, Dalcroze, or Dr. Edwin Gordon's MLT approach could signify that a teacher has both creativity and a developmental approach to teaching children. Certification in private music education programs such as Kindermusik, Music Together, Music for Young Children, Suzuki, and Yamaha let you know that a teacher will employ a reliable curriculum and excellent materials.

The teacher who holds an advanced degree or specialized certification may or may not be the one who can best inspire your child. Some very gifted teachers are self-taught or work independently, developing their own approaches to educating young musicians. Yes, training is important, but a parent can learn more about the quality of a teacher by inviting a discussion of his teaching approach. We all know when we hear the sound of enthusiasm.

Earning an advanced degree is only one way music teachers develop professional expertise. Some music teachers have pieced together their training without ever going to college.

First and foremost, find someone who has a passion for education and genuinely likes teaching youngsters. It's safest to go with someone who is not a perfectionist. Teachers who become frustrated when students make mistakes have a way of making children feel nervous, self-conscious, or discouraged. Highly perfectionistic teachers do their best work with older students, particularly those who are prodigies or play quite well, and who take their music education very seriously. The most successful perfectionistic teachers find interesting ways to inspire dedicated music students to greater heights of excellence.

Many of us have encountered a music teacher whose style could best be described as perfectionistic and demanding. Most of us are familiar with the stereotype of the music teacher who snaps at hapless children to "stand at the back and mouth the words." How easily we conjure the image of the youth orchestra director bellowing at the strings to sit up straight and play in tune. Ach, misery unbridled! But why?

For centuries, a large portion of music educators have come to teaching only as a way to earn money; their first love is performance. Others begin teaching music to children only after they've painfully relinquished their dreams of becoming world-renowned performers. People in these situations cope with a fair amount of personal, artistic, and professional frustration. After all, the competition to succeed in classical music exceeds what most normal mortals can tolerate. It is ferocious. Only a handful of musicians rise to the top, and most everyone else must settle for playing in smaller, less celebrated orchestras, local chamber groups, or professional ensembles. Not bad, but not the big time either.

If they choose to teach, such musicians typically prefer working at the high school or college level. But those who like teaching children may decide to build large private practices. The ones who become popular via the local grapevine are usually the ones who feel an affinity for children; their compassion for beginners balances that ingrained set of aesthetic standards that inspired *them* to work hard to become musicians. So I like to encourage parents of beginning music students to look for teachers with a soft touch and to avoid grouches at all costs.

A good music teacher communicates well and listens. She does not teach in a vacuum. She makes an effort to understand her students, checking in with them and exploring what they think and feel about the lesson material, their own playing, and their musical tastes. She makes learning music more personal by adapting the material, resequencing lessons, or trying new techniques when a student is ready or struggling. A good teacher is responsive.

An effective teacher has more than one trick up her sleeve. She imparts new concepts through reading and writing activities, conversing, composing, demonstrating, playing games, perhaps even moving and dancing with students as part of teaching them rhythms. She gives rewards—smiles, prizes, stickers, or stamps on children's music when they do well or try hard. She looks for what works.

An effective teacher gives a child feedback, keeping it upbeat, sensitive, constructive, and honest. She helps students end each lesson on a positive, hopeful note, empowering them to feel proud of their accomplishments, and inspiring them to practice during the week. A good teacher is genuinely supportive.

Here are some practical steps you might take in order to evaluate a potential music teacher:

- Reach the teacher by phone; ask for a face-to-face meeting. Trying to reach a teacher by phone will tell you a lot right off the bat. Is he accessible? Does he call back? Are you stuck playing phone tag for a week or more, or does he respond promptly? A request for a brochure and references will let you know if the teacher is organized, professional, and able to get information to you in a timely manner.

- In the initial phone conversation, learn as many facts as you can. Your face-to-face meeting should allow you to focus more on interpersonal style and teaching techniques than logistics.

- During your phone interview, inquire about the teacher's training, teaching methods, and expectations for students and parents. Ask about costs, rules, and payment arrangements. Gather all the basic information you can. Be sure to pay special attention to your own feelings during the phone interview, noting how comfortable or uncomfortable you felt talking with this person. (Your child may respond the same way.)

- During an in-person interview, talk with the teacher about your child's learning styles and notice if the teacher seems interested and receptive. If your child has particular learning style strengths or deficits, get a sense whether the teacher will take these into consideration. Ask the teacher questions to help you gain a better understanding of her policies, expectations, behavior management style, musical orientation, and more. Here are 21 questions to get you started.

1. What musical styles do you teach to students?

2. Do you use certain books and materials? What are they?

3. Do you always choose the music your students are learning to play or do they help?

4. At what point might you invite a child to help select music?

5. How do you address ear training in lessons?

6. How do you handle scheduling conflicts? Are you available for make-up lessons?

7. Do children sing in your class? In what context? With solfége?

8. Do your classes include games or movement activities?

9. Do children perform for each other in your class? How do you help them overcome shyness?

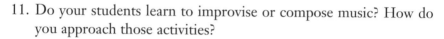

10. Do you hold recitals? How do you prepare children for them?

11. Do your students learn to improvise or compose music? How do you approach those activities?

12. Do you have any special rules for student conduct in your music lessons?

13. How do you reward student progress?

14. How do you let children know you want them to do something differently during class?

15. What is your policy and approach to practice?

16. What do you do if you think a child isn't practicing enough?

17. How do you see the parent's role in music lessons and practice?

18. How do you prefer to communicate with parents?

19. Do you give progress reports or evaluations at certain times?

20. Am I welcome to observe lessons?

21. What do you think about musical competitions?

- Observe a lesson if you can. If that is not possible, but you are inclined to sign your child up, do so for a one-time "meet and greet" experience.

*Children who
pursue musical
inquiries because
they are curious
do better and feel
better about
themselves than
children who only
aim to please
their teachers.*

- Pay special attention to the way the teacher motivates your child. Does he invite exploration or deliver instructions? Is his tone warm and congenial or strict and demanding? Does your child have choices in the lessons, or must she follow directions the whole time? Children need to be allowed to be children. Children who pursue musical inquiries because *they* are curious do better and feel better about themselves than children who only aim to please their teachers

- Note whether or not the teacher gives your child encouragement to think independently, trying out her own ideas. This helps your child take an active role in lessons and think creatively.

- Notice the manner in which the teacher offers your child feedback. Is he respectful and sensitive? Does he guide or subtly criticize? Is your child given the opportunity to make adjustments and try again? If she feels stuck, does the teacher find a different way to approach the challenge?

- In a moment when your child's attention wanders, notice how the teacher handles getting her back on track. Does she change the activity, say something engaging, or voice personal frustration?

- Will the teacher disengage from her own agenda for the lesson in response to your child's mood and readiness? On an off day (since we all have them), does the teacher relax and adjust her expectations for your child's lesson, or does she seem to push your child to work harder? Placing pressure on children to perform often has the opposite effect, especially if something is bothering the child. An experienced teacher knows this!

- After you leave the lesson, ask your child for feedback. Children may or may not be able to analyze their experiences in a lesson, but they'll know what they liked, if they felt good in general, and whether or not they want to go back.

I really appreciate my daughter's violin teacher. He's kind and very enthusiastic. I just don't understand why she complains about him. She says he won't let her do what she wants. I tell her that he knows what's best for her—he's the teacher. But she is fighting me tooth and nail, complaining that lessons are no fun. How do I get her to follow his directions, give lessons her best effort, and see where they lead her?

Developing a good working relationship between teacher and student often takes work and time, just like any other significant relationship. It helps if you start off with compatible people. But if your daughter and her teacher are not so lucky, it may be possible to improve the student-teacher rapport with everyone's effort and communication. The time for action is now—before your daughter refuses to become part of the solution.

Since you would like to see your daughter's violin lessons with this teacher succeed, you are going to have to reconcile yourself to paying attention to your daughter's complaints, even though they don't seem valid to you. Many children learn to get the attention they crave by griping. But if you decide to treat each complaint as an invitation to solve a problem, she may explore her feelings and come out with what is actually causing the problem.

Something about the pupil-teacher match is not working for your child. She might be experiencing a learning style or personality mismatch. In either case, she is missing the teacher's point because she feels that he is missing hers. Since the teacher is the adult and a paid professional, it's his job to try to work with both of you effectively. If your daughter is struggling, he needs to care about that and make some changes. If he is unwilling to work things through, then you will know for certain that it's time to find a different teacher.

I'd suggest you request a meeting or a three-way phone conference with the aim of clearing the air and developing some better communication and lesson strategies. Maybe with your help, pupil and teacher will hear

If you regard yourself as a valuable team member, ready to assist both teacher and pupil as they attempt to meet one another halfway, your daughter will feel supported and will actually start enjoying lessons more.

one another and come to an agreement. If you regard yourself as a valuable team member, ready to assist both teacher and pupil as they attempt to meet one another halfway, your daughter will feel supported and will actually start enjoying lessons more. Sometimes the relationships that start out on the wrong foot become the most cherished and valuable of all.

It's entirely possible that your daughter wants to play music that is incompatible with the teacher's approach. If the teacher can be flexible, you've got a solution. If not, your daughter may need and additional teacher or a different one in order to learn to play what she loves. See if you can help her put the sequence of her studies into perspective while out support her developing sense of aesthetics. This is bound to be a winning combination.

I'm from the old school, as they say. I was taught that teachers knew what was best.(My folks never questioned what or how the nuns taught us!) So, of course, I have never been comfortable interviewing teachers. It just feels confrontational to me. Would you please provide some examples of matching children with teachers so I have a little more information to go on?

Let's start with three-year-old Gregory and his 18-month-old sister, Becky. Gregory is old enough to enjoy a class but too young to practice a musical instrument every day. He is a highly energetic child who learns well by doing, moving, and touching—a kinesthetic-tactile learner, which is fairly common in three-year-olds and in toddlers like Becky. Greg and Becky both have difficulty doing anything that requires them to sit still and listen for more than five minutes.

Although not billed as music classes, baby gym classes can provide tiny tots with a delightful and age-appropriate introduction to music.

Obviously, private music lessons are not appropriate at this time. Greg's K-T style and young age tell us that his musical development would flourish in a music and movement class such as Music Together. He'd also love a "Mommy and me" style program that incorporates music with other activities. A physical education class like Gymboree or another baby gym program would expose him to music while he's in motion—a great combination for the K-T child. If he hears and feels the rhythms of music while moving around, he will be acquiring rhythmic awareness, integrating rhythm through large motor play, and he will associate music with having fun. Although not billed as music classes, baby gym classes can provide tiny tots with a delightful and age-appropriate introduction to music.

Next let's consider gregarious, four-year-old Tosha. This child has fabulous auditory skills. She mimics animals, plays with the full potential of her speaking and singing voices, and accurately sings songs and snippets of instrumental music she's heard only in passing. Tosha has a strong kinesthetic, tactile style as well. She takes a dance class with her mom and has always been a mess maker, enjoying activities with her whole body.

Tosha doesn't read yet, but it's not too soon to introduce her to the visual symbols of music in a playful way. In fact, because she is so auditorily gifted, it would be good to help her get acquainted with visual representations of music early on. Any young child's program that includes note-reading games and activities could get her learning to read using her auditory talents. Note and symbol flash-card games, feltboard notes, dry-erase writing, art activities with notes as images, music bingo—all these materials are fun and informative for young children. Parents interested in getting materials like these can search online under the keywords "music education supplies." Several companies offer excellent products.

Suzuki lessons could work well for Tosha. She is already good at following instructions and she enjoys being in a group of children. She has been acquiring a repertoire of gospel tunes at church, and listening to a lot of pop music on the radio. Suzuki lessons would put her auditory skills to work memorizing classical melodies she will learn to play on violin, piano, or guitar. Suzuki would also have Tosha up, moving, and getting into playing position right from the start—good activities for her kinesthetic, tactile style. Suzuki lessons would expose her to music theory as well. She might also do fine in a keyboard-based class with Music for Young Children.

Tosha does not require private lessons at this stage because she'll enjoy the social interaction of group classes. A better time to consider finding a private teacher would be when her basic musical skills are in place and she's ready for specific challenges and coaching.

Now let's consider Cheryl. She's a giggly five-year-old, a budding socialite, and full of curiosity. She is so social that it sometimes interferes with her ability to concentrate. She's a bit impulsive, too, which makes group interaction a challenge.

Cheryl learned to write her name in preschool and draws copious pictures of her world. She tied her own shoes at four, and she makes short words out of letter magnets on the refrigerator. Cheryl is certainly grapho-motoric and perhaps visual as well. But Cheryl rarely remembers what she's asked to do. Her dad asks her three times to put on her shoes and socks, find her jacket, and meet him by the front door. But he finds her ten minutes later with the shoes and socks lying on the floor in a little heap as she plays dolls. She doesn't remember the last portion of his request very clearly. The performance of her auditory sequential memory is questionable.

Cheryl also has no sense of pitch or tonal center. Her voice strays across a melody like a sheep in a blizzard. High and low have no longitude or latitude in her mind. Cheryl's weak auditory processing suggests that she may have an immature cochlea. She needs a teacher who will give her chances to write music down and play with notes and symbols on paper. She also needs that teacher to be exceptionally patient and creative in the area of ear training, teaching her to listen closely to pitches, to learn their spatial relationships, and to sing them accurately. Most of all, she needs all this to be fun or she'll lose interest. So a multimodal teaching method will work well for Cheryl, and a private teacher who can help her focus one-on-one stands the best chance of helping her learn to make music. So even though she is young, semiprivate or private lessons with someone trained in Orff might help her develop better auditory skills while she learns to make music.

Then there's Lenny, who is six. Lenny is shy. His parents hope that music classes will help draw Lenny out socially. He responds well to the structure of school, so a more formal, regimented style of music class makes sense for him. Too much freedom makes him uncomfortable and unable to focus.

Lenny wants to know what the teacher expects of him. He likes to learn one thing at a time. He hates noise and chaos. He has fair auditory skills, good visual skills, and poor grapho-motoric skills and is otherwise well coordinated but not particularly kinesthetic. We could say he is most strongly a visual learner, but in truth, he needs a hands-on experience that doesn't require much writing. He would work well with a set curriculum and some computer-assisted learning in a lab or at home. He could also do well in Kindermusik with a very structured teacher. This setting might also help him build social skills and self-confidence.

Lenny is old enough to think about the music he is making. He can read at the second-grade level already. He would probably get a lot of satisfaction from taking a keyboard class with Yamaha. He'd be with other children in an organized environment. Headphones plugged into keyboards would keep his musical world focused and personal. He'd be working on a very linear instrument with a clear set of rules. He could practice at home with computer games. He would not have to do the "Hokey-Pokey" or stand in front of his class and sing a song, both activities this child might find unapproachable. Still, a social environment would be good for Lenny. In the right situation, he might begin to overcome his shyness and connect with the other music students. With a MIDI-keyboard style class, his computer skills would not only come in handy, they could also improve.

Next, there's seven-year-old Melissa. She faces a special challenge because her eyesight is not good, and she suffered from countless ear infections when she was little. She received shunts twice already after putting up with recurring bouts of ear pain. During key periods of language acquisition, her auditory processing had been impaired and she missed learning to distinguish the subtle differences between short vowel sounds. Even now, she tends not to listen as well as she should because during the time when her ears gave her pain, she learned not to rely on them for information. She compensated by learning to read people's faces and body language. During this developmental period, she also began turning inward to a world of imagination. One might wonder about the relevance of these details, but the truth is that all of these phenomena affected her potential to learn in an academic setting, and this has, in turn, affected her self-esteem as well as her ability to learn music.

When a child has two or more learning channels impaired, she is bound to miss people's cues. She might incorrectly interpret information. Her frequent mistakes may be mistaken by uninformed individuals as a sign that she lacks intelligence. Many children have gotten shabby treatment and the wrong impression of themselves under these circumstances. But in fact, Melissa is very bright! She is both grapho-motoric and auditory, even though her auditory channel was temporarily impaired. It works now, but she hasn't learned to use it fully again. With music training, perhaps she will.

Melissa loves singing, has great auditory sequential *memory*, is exceptionally passionate about playing piano, and intuitively composes heartrending melodies. Her fine motor coordination is outstanding. She loves writing and drawing (even though her spelling is a disaster), and she plays the piano keys quite fluidly.

Because of her unique learning profile, Melissa will need to study music privately with a sensitive, auditorily oriented teacher who emphasizes playing what one hears and feels, improvising, ear training, and composing. These techniques could help Melissa open her ears up again and compensate for the time when she could not bear to listen.

This teacher cannot expect to follow a fixed curriculum or any plan he has used with other students in the past. Teaching music to Melissa will be a unique experience. In addition, the teacher will need to adapt printed materials to fit Melissa's visual deficit. He might enlarge sheet music for Melissa, and successfully teach her to warm up to reading music by writing down her compositions and playing them back according to her notes.

Melissa could also study with someone who teaches folk music by ear. Without tackling the visual component of making music, she can still be a musician. Many beloved pop musicians these days do not read music either.

Melissa is probably both the most impaired and the most talented of all the children we've discussed so far. If her parents find the right teacher and help the teacher understand Melissa's learning issues, her musicality will continue to grow and the quality of her life will improve. However, the wrong teacher could easily discourage Melissa to the point that she gives up music, simply by becoming too frustrated or self-critical. When a child's self-esteem is fragile, she really needs someone caring and compassionate on her side. A private teacher is her best bet, someone with a background in choral music.

Last but not least, let's think about Asher. He's eight and a science whiz. He is not particularly musically motivated, but he likes listening to blues music with his dad. At his family's prompting, he's willing to try music lessons for a while. He's most drawn to instruments with mechanisms and gizmos and hopes to play saxophone someday. He has a good sense of humor, a nice sense of rhythm, and a "why not?" attitude.

Asher is globally normal, meaning he has good function in each of his learning channels. His best learning channel is visual, and this is complimented by his exceptional sense of spatial relations. He could study music using any method, in a group or private lesson, with any qualified teacher, and do just fine. But Asher does his best when he feels inspired. A charismatic teacher might be just the ticket—someone whose enthusiasm rubs off on his students.

This child is a perfect candidate for guitar or for a brass instrument—one with valves or a slide and the potential to sound bluesy and jazzy. Asher will fit right into a fourth- and fifth-grade school band program. This introverted but friendly child can fit in socially with his band mates; rehearsals and performances will get him out from behind his computer after school. He may even discover that he likes performing with a group.

Establishing common musical ground with his father is a bonus. If his dad takes him to concerts, shops with him for CDs, and supports his efforts to rally a buddy or friends into a garage band, Asher's musical development will have facilitated a lot of quality time with his father. Good stuff to share during the years ahead.

Asher can become a lifelong musician. He probably won't pursue a career in music, but he will always treasure his positive experiences. From time to time he'll jam with friends and play in one context or another. One thing is for certain: Asher will never sell his horn.

Asher's parents may want to sign him up for guitar lessons at the local music store or for private instruction on the band instrument of his choice. If he wants to start playing an instrument now to prepare for band, I recommend he try recorder. He'll learn breathing and fingering techniques that he can use later on, and he'll get an introduction to reading music. When he enters fourth grade, he'll be raring to go. But of course, if he falls in love with a different instrument, you gotta respect a kid's instincts.

I want to sign my child up for a music program, but the teacher says her program requires a commitment of almost $300 and ten lessons to get started. I find this a bit intimidating, even though she seems qualified and her studio appears to be very inviting. I don't know if my son will like the classes enough to keep on going for ten weeks. Should I try to get her to agree to fewer lessons?

Some programs work through a fixed curriculum that consists of several progressive levels, each one lasting for two or three months. Students who complete one level move up to the next one. Families commit themselves to following the program from level to level, hoping their children will continue to grow musically. Teachers who offer a program like this get training, support, educational materials, and advertising help and advice from the main company. The convenience of such an affiliation makes teaching in a franchised program very attractive to some teachers. They can start a music studio in a new town, or open or reenergize a music studio in their own town, and hit the ground running. Essentially, they train in the method and become the latest purveyor of it to the public.

By signing on with a privately franchised music program, a music teacher is agreeing to meet several requirements. She is expected to administer business matters in accordance with program costs and policies. She is expected to teach by the book. This formula is meant to keep parents and kids on track. It gets everyone in the habit of purchasing new educational materials. It also ensures a modicum of quality control and consistency between programs in a variety of locations. This strategy allows your child to complete level one in Seattle, and when you move to Portland, enroll in level two there without losing a step. Great for families bound to relocate.

For children, a cookie-cutter music program can produce excellent or mediocre results. You are right to be cautious. You need more information before you commit to ten weeks of lessons. Any structured program could fit your neighbors' children perfectly, yet leave yours feeling confused or bored. But your child might just as easily be in the group of children that loves and thrives in that program.

Success for children who feel like square pegs depends largely on the ability of the teacher to adapt curriculum or deviate from the plan enough to be inclusive. This is no small task in a room full of children holding or sitting in front of musical instruments! In your situation, I recommend you ask this teacher some of the questions listed on pages 142 and 143. The teacher's responses should help you make an educated guess about her ability to adjust her program to fit your child's style.

As a baseline, we must expect that any prefab curriculum is developmentally accurate, tested, and child friendly. This way, any child stands to enjoy learning to make music in the program. If yours does not, he should be able to bow out gracefully and find different ways to learn music. If you try the class and he doesn't like it, I'd recommend getting him involved with something more appropriate as soon as possible.

Now let's look at the financial part of your situation. It's upsetting to some of us when we are asked to commit our hard-earned dollars to a program we do not know much about. It feels a little like gambling—not every parent's favorite modus operandi. Could you ask the teacher whether she'll allow you to receive a partial refund if your child wishes to drop out mid-session? A teacher's willingness to work with you probably depends on her company's policies, but some teachers have a high degree of flexibility accompanied by a sense of fairness. Most would hope for the same gracious treatment from you, if the tables were turned.

It's upsetting to some of us when we are asked to commit our hard-earned dollars to a program we do not know much about. It feels a little like gambling.

I'd start by asking the teacher for permission to drop into a class or participate in one free session. If that's not possible, see if you can pay for an initial lesson as a "meet and greet" session. Afterward, you'll have a clear idea of what you are committing to if you sign on that dotted line.

Chapter 14

Practice, Progress, and Reinforcements

When I was a young kid, my parents and I constantly argued about practicing in between my music lessons. How can I avoid falling into the same trap with my own children?

Practice has caused more controversy between parent and child, child and teacher, and teacher and parent than any other aspect of music education. All too often, the arguments that arise single-handedly steal the joy right out of our children's music education. Fortunately, practice can be structured and conducted in a much more productive manner.

That's where we come in. Since the teacher cannot come home with our children and look over their shoulders, it's up to us to make sure the home link is effective. We can see what's going on during our children's practice sessions and use our common sense to make a few adjustments. Getting involved with children's musical practice can turn it into a pleasant, positive experience instead of the old nag-and-whine routine!

Let's begin with some essential considerations of how children function in a practice situation. For young children, age six and below, there are two schools of thought regarding musical practice. One school says that youngsters should participate in musical play, creativity, and the process of discovery, refraining from musical practice until they are older. With this approach, practice is eliminated in favor of engaging in musical play during the class and at home.

Getting involved with children's musical practice can turn it into a pleasant, positive experience instead of the old nag-and-whine routine!

At some point, every music student needs to get down to business.

It's true that most young children flourish without a lot of structure. They like playing, changing focus, exploring one thing and then another. Young children rarely engage in one activity for more than a few minutes, so formal practice can feel too rigid. For developmental reasons, giving a practice routine to a very young child is likely to cause a temper tantrum, followed by lengthy battle of the wills. Trouble is, regular practice is the only thing that will help a child develop musical ability beyond the most basic instrumental skills. So taking the playful exposure approach will only work for very young children, and not for very long. At some point, every music student needs to get down to business.

Another school of thought about early childhood music practice is that children should begin practicing as early as three years of age, with a parent functioning as partner and guide. This gets children in the habit and keeps them from feeling isolated or straying off course. In early childhood, a parent's role in a practice session must be one of positive, total engagement.

Starting children on any educational pursuit at such a young age is controversial. It falls into the same category as showing math flash cards to babies. You either like the notion of early training or you hate it.

Parents might argue that some children are able to stay focused as young as two or three, therefore they see a point in getting kids into music classes that early. Some would recall that Mozart, that incomparable genius, was already playing two instruments and composing dances by age five. All right, there are a few kids who absolutely crave training before they are out of diapers. And if they are truly prodigious and ready to learn, they should have the opportunity. But pushing children to achieve before they have any sense of themselves has major consequences psychologically. If you are going to take the path of early study and early practice, I hope you will keep your eyes and ears open for signs of stress and be prepared to take time off if your child needs a break. Remember—children feel better about themselves when they accomplish something *they* care about. Learning to do something because you tell them to may build skills but it may also leave their deeper sense of pride gasping for breath.

If you want to start your child with music lessons before age six, ask the teacher for ideas about making practice into parent-child play. If you attempt musical practice a few times and give the teacher feedback each week, you can refine your practice process as you go. If you'd like to learn more about parental involvement in practice, I recommend reading the work of Shinichi Suzuki. He pioneered the practice of mother and child playing music together.

It's important to consider that taking a central role in your child's musical encounters can ask you to wear two hats—those of parent and musical guide. To preserve the fun and good-natured spirit of the latter role, it helps to relinquish some of the authority that comes with the former!

My child is six years old and seems ready to take lessons that require practice. How much is really appropriate?

This depends entirely on your child. If yours is a butterfly flitting from flower to flower to experience all the colors and possibilities, lessons that require structured practice may be challenging to both of you. Putting such a free-spirited child into structured lessons prematurely may backfire. If yours fits this description, you might consider staying with classes and fun music-inclusive activities for another year.

On the other hand, you may be noticing that your child thrives on structure. At six, he could very well be able to embark on a course of sequential musical study that includes practice. Many music instruction programs such as Suzuki or Music for Young Children take this approach, incorporating fun activities and worksheets to do at home under the banner of practice. In this case, a practice schedule of 15 to 20 minutes a day is reasonable.

Signs that your child is ready to practice regularly include the ability to:

- Follow a schedule;

- Focus for ten to fifteen minutes on a single activity;

- Follow verbal and written directions;

- Perform and complete little homework assignments and tasks on time;

- Recognize mistakes and make an attempt to correct them;

- Repeat tasks in order to perfect them.

Once you've determined that your child is mature enough, you can start working on building the amount of time he spends doing just that. I start children at age four and five with a goal of practicing (play-time style) for ten minutes. Once they have succeeded at this consistently, we add five minutes to the practice sessions. Children can make progress with as few as three practice sessions a week when they are young and just getting started. But if children are enjoying practice a great deal, it's fine to include it in their daily routine. Typically, once children adjust to a full school day schedule in the first grade, they may be able to handle practicing for fifteen to twenty minutes a day. Practice sessions for young children should last no more than thirty minutes.

We are wise to take our children's school homework into consideration when deciding how long and how often they ought practice. Weekly homework is normal in first and second grade and hardly conflicts with musical practice. By third grade, a more significant amount of homework may be assigned every night.

Since children need time to space out, cuddle, snack, and goof off, parents should not feel pressed to enforce a rigorous musical practice schedule every day. You've got to read your kids and go from there. If they can handle a short period of practice time daily (ten minutes) and still fit their school homework in without feeling overloaded, then that is what makes sense at your house. When we add on afterschool enrichment, sports, or clubs, we must be careful to strike a balance so our children do not strike out!

Children benefit from being important participants in setting their own musical goals and expectations. A child who wants to work hard will need your help figuring out how to set up a livable schedule that includes more musical practice. (In first grade, this would be unusual but not unheard of.)

A child who wants to work hard will need help figuring out how to set up a livable schedule that includes more musical practice.

To decide how much practice time suits your child, ask his teacher for guidelines, and try to follow them for a week. Your child's energy is a good indicator of how long he can practice effectively. You can shorten or lengthen sessions accordingly. (Many parents find giving their children a high-protein snack before practicing helps sustain their energy and attention.)

In our busy lives, we often forget to reflect on how things are going. Yet reflection and discussion are absolutely essential tools for learning and living well. We can teach our children to reflect about their lives when we take time out to talk together. So as you refine your child's practice routine, be sure to openly discuss how he feels about it. Help him be specific. Focus on details as well as results. Then you can bring your questions and suggestions to the teacher at the next lesson. Together you can make adjustments so that practice itself is a pleasure!

Why don't children like to practice their instruments at home as often as parents and music teachers want them to?

The most common reason kids do not want to practice their musical instruments between lessons is because everyone expects them to. Practice becomes an obligation that feels weighty. Any act children perform under those conditions is much less enjoyable simply because someone is expecting them to perform it. They anticipate and dread the consequences of disappointing others. They start telling themselves they "should" do this, they "ought to" do that, but they'd rather not. They begin to feel chained to adults' hopes and expectations. The point of practice can altogether disappear under a cloud of duty. Kids begin feeling that they might as well make their beds, set the table, and take out the trash. (Sounds like real life to this mom.)

If children are told to "practice or else," they'll do so out of fear of losing our approval or relinquishing some cherished privilege. This will damage their musical motivation and teach them to associate making music with family conflict. If you find yourself ready to level a threat over musical practice, cool off and call the teacher instead. Ask for support and expert advice. You'll be glad you did not back yourself and your child into an unfriendly corner.

When we try to use *guilt* to motivate kids to practice, it can cause resentment. We tell them to practice because they made a commitment to us, and we spent good money on their instrument and lessons. So they heave a sigh and go back to work, their musical endeavors feeling like a form of servitude. Guilt is just as insidious as fear as a motivational tool.

For some particularly oppositional kids, parental threats just make them dig their heels in deeper. Refusing to practice can become a somewhat perverted attempt to preserve self-respect. If you are already locked into this dynamic with a child, it's time to ask for help from a parenting education or counselor.

Of course, we have to do something to make sure our children practice. If we say nothing, they may not practice at all! So we face this age-old bind. Many parents of the masters did, too. (Of course some of them could have attributed their children's successes to the fact that corporal punishment was not considered legal grounds for losing possession of one's children.)

Yes, some children are intrinsically motivated to practice. Not all provoke parental badgering. One friend reports that her teenage daughter began practicing her instrument like crazy as soon as she was told she didn't have to. She practiced because the decision was all hers.

Short of letting our kids take music lessons without making a commitment to working between lessons, what can we do to motivate them to practice more? We can help make practice more fun and meaningful than sitting alone performing repetitive exercises. For ideas along these lines, please read on.

Lately I find myself commanding my daughter to practice. I hear myself barking at her to "get busy." But this feels awful to me. She's a good kid and she likes her music lessons, but lately she is slacking off. How can I get us both back on track?

First off, let's slow down and back up. If you are shouting orders, something in your daughter's musical situation isn't quite right. I suggest you assist her, calmly and quietly, to develop a practice routine and a schedule she can feel good about. With an improved routine and schedule in place, you'll both be clear about her practice goals and you'll have a basis for working out the details. This will require a discussion about how things are going. Perhaps in the course of conversation, some underlying challenge may become visible. Once you have come up with new ways to address it and practice, she'll have a more acceptable plan, one to which she feels committed and accountable.

We are so excited. Our third grader is starting clarinet lessons and we want to set up a nice practice area for her. Our apartment is kind of cramped, plus she has two brothers—one older and one toddler—so we are feeling a little spatially challenged. What will help her do well and feel good about practicing? P.S. She may need glasses.

Covering the basics together before your child embarks on a practice routine will really help her succeed.

It's important to plan or assess any practice environment. Children benefit from having adequate light, quiet, and a workable space in order to practice. They need to be able to retrieve their music from a handy storage spot. They may need a tape recorder, a special stool, or a music stand. Keeping those things at hand but out of the way can take a little figuring out. Use corners, hidden storage, and ingenuity!

Second, make sure your daughter's health will support her practice efforts. Children's eyes and visual processing must be in good working order if reading music is part of the plan. If your daughter seems to be having a vision problem of some kind, practice will be difficult. Annual eye exams will help ensure that your young musician can see the printed page clearly. If your child complains of eyestrain or headaches, be sure to visit a developmental optometrist and encourage her to take five- to ten-minute breaks in the middle of her practice sessions. Prolonged reading may be getting the best of her energy. During these breaks she should rest her eyes and refrain from reading, watching television, or sitting in front of a computer screen. She can also switch from reading music to other musical activities such as playing by ear or practicing scales she knows by heart.

If your child complains of eyestrain or headaches, be sure to visit a developmental optometrist and encourage her to take five- to ten-minute breaks in the middle of her practice sessions.

If your child sees reversals, or frequently loses her place in music during practice or lessons, she may be having a problem coordinating the muscles in her eyes. In this case, she should see a developmental optometrist who is capable of analyzing each subtle muscle function. If her cognitive processing of visual information is causing the difficulty with reading music, she probably has a similar problem with normal reading. If this is the case, you can obtain helpful information and support from the International Dyslexia Society, accessible online. If her difficulty in reading music has to do with interpreting or recalling the spatial relationships between symbols and notes, she might have a spatial-analytic deficit that can be treated with integration of educational therapeutic techniques into music lessons. None of these experiences should keep children from becoming comfortable reading music. Each challenge can be reduced or overcome.

Next, let's consider the time of day your daughter will practice. Sometimes when musicians switch the time of day when they practice, they find that their concentration and energy improve. Just because afternoon practice seems to make sense with a child's school schedule doesn't mean her biorhythms can cooperate. If she's an early riser, practicing for fifteen minutes in the morning before school could turn out to be more positive and productive than thirty minutes spent struggling against fatigue at the end of the day.

After-school practice can work for many children. Healthy food is a key ingredient for making afternoon practice a productive experience for kids. Nutritionists recommend a high-protein snack right after school. Avoid sugary treats and carbohydrate loading. These only make your child's energy soar, then crash a short time later, turning the rest of the afternoon into a cranky or spacey mope. Instead, offer cheese and crackers, peanut butter on celery or whole wheat bread, or a smoothie with a protein boost and banana added for potassium. Any of these snacks or others you might dream up should raise your daughter's energy and concentration into moderate gear.

If your child is a night owl and a would-be late sleeper, your best options are either practicing right after dinner or just before bed. (After dinner can be a family audience time if your child wants company.) Nighttime practice can give working parents the chance to share in their child's musical life. But keeping distractions to a minimum is key at this hour. If possible, unplug or ignore the phone and turn the TV and radio off. If your practicing child wants some privacy, try to accommodate her wishes by keeping siblings busy in other activities. Even if you don't have the space to separate the children, keeping those who are not practicing focused on drawing or a book can

Healthy food is a key ingredient for making afternoon practice a productive experience for kids.

be almost as good. (Nothing interrupts a child's practice faster than a critical comment from a brother or sister.)

In your situation, I might resort to the divide-and-conquer approach. Have a plan at practice time for big brother to take little brother for a walk, or one of you parents can take them both out for ice cream.

A nice way to end practice before bed is with a brief family musical experience such as a one-song sing-along or a parent-child duet (although you or your spouse might wind up being shooshed).

My son has been complaining that practice is "too hard." I don't understand why. The teacher gives him exercises to play that he has already learned in lessons. They don't seem hard for him to play then. What do you think is going on?

You are wondering exactly what is "too hard" about practicing. Good question. It may not be the music.

Practice has always been challenging for kids. But today's culture makes it even less attractive than ever before. Our children contend with a virtual snowstorm of media information in their daily environments. These days, images and ideas are presented to children in fast-paced eye-capturing narratives complete with loveable characters, song, and dance! All our children have to do is click the power button and channel selector on their remotes to plug in. Simply put, television, video, and DVD entertainment and edutainment are hard acts to follow. By comparison, practicing can feel like a chore. When your son complains that practice is too hard, maybe he is comparing it to watching his favorite shows. No fair.

This doesn't mean you have to blow up your TV to get him focused on productive activities. But keeping the situation in perspective and enforcing a constructive practice routine could help him learn to do the same. It's one of those times he needs to accept your wisdom and trust your authority. Eventually he will see the reasons behind your rules. When children practice in a positive way, they come to understand the

For children who crave contact with a parent, musical practice can feel like a period of enforced exile.

benefits as evidenced by their own emerging talent. Tell him he's going "unplugged."

However, there could be some very justifiable reasons your son feels that practice is too hard. You may be able to get to the source if you are willing to play detective and negotiator. For many children, practicing independently is too hard to manage, or it makes them feel lonely. So when we diminish the importance or ignore their complaints, our attitude just compounds the problem. He may just need you to hang out, listen, and care.

For children who crave contact with a parent, musical practice can feel like a period of enforced exile. Your son may not have the emotional awareness or expressiveness to tell you that he feels this way. He wouldn't be the first child to think of himself as acting "babyish" for wanting your company. But all the same, being alone with his instrument might give him an empty feeling inside. The solution, of course, is simple. Be there. Help him build independence just three minutes at a time.

It could be that sitting and focusing at a particular time of day is "too hard." Maybe his energy runs low at that hour. He could just need a snack or a rest before continuing. Afternoon is typically a harder time to focus. A healthy, high-protein snack eaten one half hour before practice could provide him with the boost he needs.

Cumulative eyestrain after several hours at school can also be the culprit. Does your son complain of headaches? If so, he could have sore eyes. You can have his eyes tested to see if he needs glasses, vision therapy, or a change in how or where his printed music is presented. Some students benefit from having their music enlarged to make it easier to read— a little extra work at the photocopy machine, but well worth the effort.

Maybe it *is* the music. Sometimes when children complain that practice is "too hard," they feel thrown by new or overly challenging material. The teacher may have expected your son to make headway with the music, but if he's experiencing trouble retaining some of what the teacher instructed during the lesson, playing alone will prove disappointing and frustrating. This is fairly common. Without sufficient information, a child will grow confused. (Tape recording lessons and playing them back during practice decreases this problem.) Working on his own, a child who feels lost will typically decide to gloss or skip over assignments. This could leave him feeling angry at the teacher or himself, and guilty for not knowing how to do what was expected. Under these circumstances, it's understandable that a child will shut down and try to beg off practice.

Again, the solution is simple. Be there. If you notice a problem, help him decide what to do. Then call the teacher. But if your work schedule prevents you from being there, arrange for another caring adult to take charge. Even a qualified babysitter can notice what goes smoothly and what does not. He or she can take notes for you, and give you feedback when you get home. Provide the training, take time to listen to the feedback, *then* call the teacher.

When we empower our children to work with us to create solutions to their problems, we are respecting their intelligence and resourcefulness.

We also hear complaints when children who've been humming along with their lessons suddenly hit an obstacle in their own playing. Sometimes their fingers just won't do what their brain tells them to. When this happens, you can expect to hear some moaning and groaning. They felt confident before and now they are faltering. What they thought was "easy" isn't. Thankfully, this frustration will resolve if you call your child's music teacher for a between-lessons phone consultation. The teacher may suggest that you reduce the amount of time your child focuses on the hard stuff. Or your child will be told to try the task differently. With one well-considered change in a practice routine, he may be able to diffuse his frustration and carry on.

If your son's complaining persists, he may need a different kind of instruction. This is worth exploring if other interventions haven't worked. It could also be time to assess your son's interest in playing this particular instrument. Maybe he feels drawn to something else—sports or another extracurricular activity. You might choose to release the instructional strand of music to make room for baseball season or chess club. If so, rest assured that it's possible to make that transition without losing a musical step. You can just make a point to pick up the self-discovery and experiential strands at home to continue braiding.

In each line of inquiry you pursue to find out what's "too hard," you can encourage your son to explore and express his thoughts and feelings. This is really positive parenting. When we empower our children to work with us to create solutions to their problems, we are respecting their intelligence and resourcefulness. Their involvement in the process imparts and strengthens three invaluable life skills: communication, problem solving, and decision making.

My son seems to finish his practice in record time. I ask if he's done everything and he says, "Yes!" So today I eavesdropped while he was practicing. He was rushing through every exercise! He made a lot of mistakes, but he didn't slow down to correct himself even once. He just kept flipping pages at 90 m.p.h. Is there something I can do to encourage him to take more time?

Lucky for your son that your ear was on the door. Far too often, we hear the first notes of our child's practice then hurry off to make a dent in our own endless list of tasks. I commend your suspicious mind.

Rushing through practice is a sign that your child is not creatively engaged in learning to play music when he is alone. You are describing someone who gives tasks he doesn't care about nothing more than a cursory pass. I'd guess he does the same thing at school. Does his teacher write "careless errors" on his papers? Fragmented sentences, missing punctuation, and sloppy work can all be signs of a child who rushes through his thoughts without taking the trouble to write them down completely. Does he bring home math tests on which he should have gotten an A but didn't? Is he a speed-reader with mediocre comprehension? It all boils down to the same thing. This kind of rushing often indicates giftedness, boredom, or both.

Many music teachers ask speedy students to practice with a metronome, a device that keeps time at specific tempos. They assign slow tempos by number for each piece of music a child practices. They also write directions like "play slowly" on the music.

While these strategies may help somewhat, I'd recommend resorting to tactics that work at a deeper level. First, see if your son is bored and needs a different approach to instruction—something more creative and less rote. Work with the teacher on making practice more challenging, adventurous, and interesting for your son.

Since kids' energy tends to run high and express itself in bursts of frenetic movement, they can find it very frustrating to take things slowly. Have you considered getting your son involved in a martial art such as tai chi or aikido? These disciplines instill a respect for the power of intense, slow movement and total concentration. Particularly with children, these kinds of self-control are naturally learned through the body. Once he can move slowly, with intention, he should be able to transfer this knowledge to his hands as he plays music.

Tackling boredom is a separate issue. When children feel things are taking too long, they may disengage and begin to carelessly rush. We need to make practice exciting so that slowing down won't feel like going to sleep. To accomplish this, you can resequence practice activities, place time limits on each one, and work with a kitchen timer and stickers to make time fly.

First, review the teacher's practice punch list with your son before he begins to play. Make sure he feels able to perform each task. Strike any from the list that seem too hard, and alert the teacher about the unwanted portions of the practice assignment before the next music lesson. This gives the teacher valuable feedback and lets her know that you are involved and ready to help.

If there are problems with the routine, you can help your son establish new, more achievable goals for practicing. You can accomplish this if you fill out the following form together, then practice everything in the order your child has written or dictated it. Anything harder is preceded and followed by an activity that releases your child from stress and builds confidence. The form is easy to complete with your child at the beginning of the week. Just ask him to finish the sentences by filling in the blanks. (If you write down the answers for him, he'll feel supported and connected to you.) When you allow your son's preferences and feelings to shape his practice routine, he'll feel more motivated and ultimately more satisfied with the outcome.

Once you have an acceptable practice routine listed on paper, your son will be ready to practice. First, place the clock or timer within his reach. Seeing the practice time pass in three- to five-minute chunks of time motivates children to continue, and reassures them that practice will soon be over. Second, place the practice sheet for the week before your child. Third, work through each activity on the sheet for the assigned amount of time using the kitchen timer. (Adjust times based on what seems to be working best.) Fourth, award your child with a star or sticker that he can place next to each listed activity or exercise as he completes it. Before he knows it, practice will be over and he will feel great.

Finally, help your child assess how well he met his overall practice goals. When he feels proud of himself and notices improvement in his playing, you'll both know you've done something right.

My Practice Goals   Date_____

1. Something I play well on my musical instrument is _____
   _____

2. Today I want to practice _____

3. Something that I'd like to play with greater ease is _____
   _____

4. A scale or exercise that is easy for me to play is _____
   _____ I'll play this next.

5. A scale or exercise that I find a bit challenging is _____

6. A musical game or activity I enjoy is _____
   _____

7. My most challenging goal for this practice session is _____
   _____

8. A piece I like and know by heart is _____

9. I want to finish practicing with a fun "free choice" activity.
   I choose: (circle one)

   a piece of music   a musical game

   improvisation   a musical story

In these hectic times, it can be hard to resist the temptation to take twenty minutes during practice to check in with your best friend for a quick phone conversation, pick up your email, or deal with bills. Sure, you need to get those things done. But if you continue to take an active role in planning and monitoring your child's practice, you'll keep abreast of his progress and demonstrate that his music education is high on your list of priorities. Why not take advantage of his need for your presence? Slow down, sip some tea, relax and listen. Don't you deserve a break?

My daughter wants a new bicycle, and my wife told her if she does well with her piano lessons, we'll think about getting it for her. Somehow, this doesn't sit well with me. I'd rather she practice because she cares about doing well. A co-worker of mine rewards his child with money when he scores goals for his soccer team. He swears it's improving his son's game. But I don't like the idea of bribing kids. What do you think of rewarding kids with money or prizes?

Enticing children to work harder in order to win prizes or money can make their experience of learning to play an instrument feel about as dignified as doing dog tricks. Mixing music with commerce is what professional musicians come to in adulthood! No need to start now. Making music can and should be its own reward.

Children, like adults, find magic in the arts through creative self-expression, not by reaching goals and getting rewards from parents and teachers. The quality of each musical experience exists in what the child thinks, feels, tries, and learns, not in what he or she receives as a bonus prize. Best save that approach for soothing kids after they get a shot or go to the dentist.

Still, we need to know how to help kids get on track and stay there. If the instrument, teacher, method, setting, and practice routine are all fine-tuned, rewarding a child in external ways shouldn't be necessary. Yet there are times when something is off and we want to encourage some stick-to-it-iveness. Doing that without resorting to bribes takes careful consideration (which is exactly why so many parents cave in under pressure). We want to draw an important distinction between rewarding a child and giving that child a sense of rewarding herself.

Parents and children can participate together to make a music portfolio— a collection of writings, photos, artwork, poetry, ticket stubs, video tapes, cassette recordings, doodles, sticker books, and diary entries created by the child about her own musical process.

Parents who find themselves resorting to bribes should ask themselves this basic question: Is my child playing to please me, or because she feels personally enriched by the experience? If your answer is *both*, the end result for your child might be musical success plus a sense of being a "good" daughter. This is very normal. There's nothing wrong with your child doing something because it makes you proud or happy. But that alone won't turn her into a creative, committed musician. That requires a strong personal connection to the music.

Children who play to please do not play forever. Eventually, when parents stop reinforcing their musical efforts with rewards, they realize the music doesn't mean that much to them and they decide to quit playing. (Sadly, that's normal, too.)

One thing parents can do to make music more personally rewarding for children is to teach them *how* to care about the quality of their own musical efforts. Introducing them to the process of self-assessment can make a difference.

Assessment means measurement or evaluation. We usually think of tests and grades when we hear these words, but assessment does not mean either one in this case. The concept behind self-assessment involves gaining a sense of one's accomplishments by noticing and celebrating significant moments and improvements. Kids can do this in fun, creative, and meaningful ways by creating a personal music portfolio.

Parents and children can participate together to make a music portfolio—a collection of writings, photos, artwork, poetry, ticket stubs, video tapes, cassette recordings, doodles, sticker books, and diary entries created by the child about her own musical process. The portfolio makes the child's musical experiences tangible and puts them in chronological order.

How to create a portfolio? You might start with a photo album, scrapbook, or large artist's portfolio. Begin by taking photos of your child making music. Invite your child to take photos of her favorite musical things and places. Add photos of family music experiences—going to a concert, singing together, listening to a marching band at a parade, anything musical will add value to the portfolio. (It helps to keep a loaded camera at the ready!) Save concert and event ticket stubs, recital programs, letters from grandparents that refer to music, any document or treasure that relates to your child's musical interest.

Then at least once every couple of weeks, take a few minutes with your child to write, draw, paint, or make a collage together about music. She can dictate to you or write independently about music lessons, pieces of music she has heard or played, or ideas she's having. Incorporate all the recent musical goodies into your child's musical portfolio. List favorite songs and CDs. Encourage her to add magazine pictures of musical artists she likes. Everything and anything goes, the more the better.

A music portfolio can work magic. When the chips are down, your child can look over her drawings, read the poems and musings, count the completed sticker charts, watch the home video, laugh at the photos, share the memories, and recall all the reasons she likes making music. Chances are excellent that keeping and reviewing a music portfolio will constantly renew your child's commitment to making music. It also makes it easy for your child to share her musical experiences with friends and relatives.

I find my son responds well to reward systems, and I'd like to start one regarding his practice schedule. Do you have any guidelines for doing this?

If done appropriately, a healthy reward system can instill good habits in children. The rewards may not increase their desire to become creative, but they can promote day-to-day success in music lessons. When children actively participate in creating their own reinforcements or choosing how they mark their own successes, they should feel integral to the process rather than being demeaned or controlled by it. This can be good for your son's self-esteem. He can help himself learn to follow through.

Rewards can be used to build and reinforce a child's ongoing accomplishments during a lesson or practice session. They can bolster his morale and keep him engaged. For example, a teacher or parent can

Once your child has successfully reached his own weekly practice goal, he can set it for another week to reinforce his success. After two weeks, help him make a new plan to reach a more challenging goal.

incorporate characters such as stuffed animals or puppets into a lesson or practice session. "They" can compliment your child for tasks well done , and for having a positive attitude. My son's teacher piles Beanie Babies to the right of his music and flies them over his head when he does well, landing them in an increasingly large pile on the other side. This makes him smile and keep going. Again, the motivation is not personal and internal. But it pleases him. He plays because he wants to and the reinforcements cheer him on.

Another local teacher has a bear puppet and a bunny puppet talk to students about their work during music lessons. These light touches can make hearing feedback into a more playful experience. Counselors sometimes use puppets to help young children understand their experiences by demonstrating what they might be feeling. They can be used to boost social and emotional development, and encourage good musical habits, too.

In addition to reinforcements, here are a couple of useful techniques that will help you impart desirable habits and behaviors to your son. First, with your child, discuss and set one particular musical goal to accomplish each week, such as practicing for ten minutes each day. Once you are both clear on the goal, help your child discuss anything that might make it a challenge to accomplish. Then you'll both be ready to follow through. Begin to mark your child's daily progress with a chart, marble jar, or other system, as discussed below.

Once your child has successfully reached his own weekly practice goal, he can set it for another week to reinforce his success. After two weeks, help him make a new plan to reach a more challenging goal. Perhaps his first goal is to practice every day. His next goal might be to play more slowly, or to try playing in time to a metronome. He can always go back to reinforce the first goal again if he feels his is beginning to backslide. Notice that your are supporting his goal to "reach for the stars" instead of telling him what he needs to improve. Very different approach, very different results.

Here are two popular reward systems that are simple to set up and maintain. When children participate in these systems, and especially when they succeed, you'll have wonderful opportunities to snap photos for their music portfolio!

The Marble Jar

This kindergarten chestnut still works like a charm. Buy a bag or two of marbles. With your child, select a large glass jar she likes (no lid required), and place it in a safe, highly visible location near where your child plays her instrument or next to her bed.

Before she starts to play, break down your child's practice routine into isolated tasks such as review, scales, pieces of music, written homework, and improvisation. Sequence the practice items well. (If you'd like help formatting a practice session, please flip back to the chart titled "My Practice Goals" on page 168.) Move through the practice list, and with each completed task, invite your child to choose a new marble and drop it into the jar. (This reinforces the sense that she is in charge of her own process and progress.) You can amplify her pride by making observant comments such as, "You look very pleased!" You can ask her how she feels after she has completed challenging tasks. Your comments will help her tune into her own reactions to each experience and verbalize what she learned. She'll feel very supported by you.

After a few weeks, when the jar is full, show your child that she has earned a privilege or a prize. Take time to ask her to name at least five musical things she can do now that she could not do when the jar was empty. Name and discuss her improvements with the family! Then you can feel free to honor her commitment to music by inviting her to choose a family event. Offer her a special date with the parent of

Move through the practice list, and with each completed task, invite your child to choose a new marble and drop it into the jar.

her choice, or a turn to choose a movie to rent; you might let her pick a restaurant to celebrate her practice victory. All these rewards give her freedom to choose, recognition in the family, and something to show and remember for her efforts. But they are only valuable if she knows just what she has accomplished. This is the real reward. She does the work, she picks the prize, and she knows she has earned a sense of pride.

The Sticker Chart

The sticker chart technique is used everywhere because it reinforces behavioral change with something a child can see, touch, peel, and enjoy. Stickers are fun for children of all ages.

Create a blank calendar chart or use a paper calendar for this project. Set a practice goal for the week and write it down next to the calendar. On each day that your child meets his practice goal, allow him to choose a sticker and place it on the practice calendar in the correct spot. Each sticker he adds gets him closer to reaching his practice goal for the week.

When he practices four or five days in a row, or every other day throughout the week (remember, you set the parameters together), celebrate together. Ask him to tell you what he feels he is able to do better now. Make sure he notices a few changes in his playing each week.

Ask him to tell you what he feels he is able to do better now. Make sure he notices a few changes in his playing each week.

You can also celebrate his consistent effort with a treat or special activity. If your son also sets a monthly practice goal and reaches that, your family might enjoy celebrating with a special outing such as a movie, a trip to the zoo, or a picnic at the beach or park. Remember, helping your child see his progress in terms of his blossoming musical skills is critical to the success of using a sticker chart, a marble jar, or any other system for positive reinforcement. Even if you give rewards, treats, and privileges, the power of positive reinforcement is only as lasting as your child's insights and intrinsic motivation.

Chapter 15

Preparing to Perform

My nine-year-old has her second recital coming up in a month. At the first one she was so nervous she blanked out after 30 seconds and froze at the piano. She seems mortified it will happen again. Is there anything we can do to help her?

There are four keys to a successful performance. Know your music backward and forward, get enough sleep, eat well, and know how to calm yourself down and focus. Growing calm may be the hardest part, but relaxation and focusing techniques can be learned, even by children.

Yoga teaches us to breathe deeply and slowly. Enrolling your daughter in a yoga class for children could give her some wonderful tools for relieving her own anxiety. Yoga helps many people learn to create a sense of peace within themselves in a minute's time. (Most counselors for children also know how to lead a guided relaxation.)

Meditation tapes are also helpful and can be easily obtained. These typically talk listeners through a process of deep, focused breathing that leads into a guided meditation. Your daughter could listen just to the first section of this sort of tape. Or, if you want to learn how to coach her to breathe and center, you can copy what you hear the meditation guide say on tape. It's crucial to speak slowly and softly when you lead a meditation.

Relaxation breathing techniques are widely accepted. Breathing in slowly through one's nose for the count of three should fill your child's lungs with clean air. Exhaling through the mouth slowly for the count of three will help her to relax. This breathing in and out, nose then mouth, done at a slow, steady pace eventually creates a deep sense of calm. It can prevent or reverse that light-headed feeling and the jitters kids get at the last minute waiting to perform. It allows them to take control of their feelings and their situation.

To deepen the relaxation, meditation guides sometimes instruct people to breathe into and out of each part or region of the body, beginning in the feet and working up through the body to the top of the head. This feels great. It can calm children in any situation and can help even a highly restless child to drift off to dreamland. But it may be more than your daughter wants or needs to prepare to perform. An abbreviated version in which she fills her body and hands with breath, then "hears" the music in her mind, may suffice nicely. If your daughter learns to measure and slow her breathing while she visualizes/audiates her music, then she will feel practically unshakable and very centered on stage. From this resolve, she should be free to play what she knows and feels.

Some children also find they can calm, center, and encourage themselves by silently repeating an affirmation to boost confidence. Positive messages such as "I am a good musician" or "I like myself the way I am" may help relieve emotional stress. Musical affirmations such as "My fingers know the way" or "I allow the music to guide my hands" can help children focus on what they are about to play.

A full routine begins with your child breathing deeply before taking the stage. When she takes her place before the audience, she then helps herself to a moment of silence when she sits with her instrument with her eyes closed. This puts her in charge and gives the audience a second to quiet down, too. In this moment, she can breathe and audiate her music or remember her affirmation. Once she feels ready, she can open her eyes and begin her performance with a genuine smile. Somehow, audiences naturally seem to appreciate and respect such concentration in children; they respond to the mood that centering brings to the room.

If your daughter is facing a particularly daunting passage of music during her performance, she might consider adding one more step to her preparation. Research suggests that visualizing a perfect performance can be just as effective as participating in an actual, physical practice. So during the moments your daughter concentrates on breathing, she could visualize herself playing those challenging lines of the music with total ease.

One note of caution—your concern for her may actually add to her worries. If she feels that you are nervous for her, she could feel she also has *you* to take care of. You might try some deep breathing yourself and then you'll both feel better.

Chapter 16

Degrees of Excellence

My eight-year-old grandson feels very passionate about making music. He sings all the time and usually practices violin without being reminded. Even though his tone is still shrill and scratchy, I tell him how great he sounds. I pay for his lessons, attend his recitals, and am so proud of how hard he tries. I want him to have every chance to develop into an accomplished musician, and I am willing to cover any expenses involved. Can you think of anything special I might do to help my grandson realize his musical potential?

You are certainly a fairy grandmother! I hope you realize that you are already doing a wonderful job of supporting him. He is more than lucky to have you in his life.

Sometimes children need very little encouragement to flourish in the arts. Some successful professional musicians I know credit their families with being loving, but staying fairly uninvolved with their musical development. Children who care as much about music as your grandson does tend to make the most of whatever they are given. If you continue to provide him with music lessons and offer praise when the music sounds good, you'll be taking care of the basics.

You are more than his patron. You are also his witness. It's great that you attend his recitals and school concerts and keep a watchful eye on how his lessons are progressing. If you notice his excitement waning,

Children enjoy sharing their hobbies with other like-minded children. Your grandson's interest in making music could become the basis for a meaningful, constructive friendship.

you take him out to lunch and have a chat about how he likes his lessons. If you detect a note of discontent, explore!

Perhaps you feel you would like to get more involved with your grandson's musical life. How about purchasing tickets to the symphony for the two of you? If you're feeling generous, invite him to bring a friend. Children enjoy sharing their hobbies with other like-minded children. Your grandson's interest in making music could become the basis for a meaningful, constructive friendship. How about sharing your favorite albums from 40 years ago with him? Or if you're both readers, why not go to the library together once a month to share books about music and musicians? While you're there, find some recordings to borrow, then listen to them together.

Every child deserves to be spoiled a little by a grandmother or grandfather. To mark a very important occasion, you might see if you can take your grandson on a trip to a big city to see a Broadway musical. Perhaps you could even help him choose a special summer program for young musicians and then visit him there. A list of well-established, highly regarded summer music programs and camps is provided in "Resources."

Owning a high-quality instrument can also make a world of difference to a sensitive musician. Few families with young children can afford to purchase expensive musical instruments. Perhaps your grandson is currently playing on a student model that leaves a lot to be desired. This is normal and fine for children who are just beginning to play. But if your grandson's dedication to violin continues, you could decide to buy him a better one.

Of course, it is possible to do entirely too much. We all know people who brag every chance they get, press their little prodigies to show off, audition, and compete, and make a fuss over small accomplishments. In short, stage moms and dads can drive their kids absolutely nuts! Although grandparents get away with bragging a little more, boasting and unwanted attention can make children want to run and hide. So if you feel a questionable urge to brag, do whatever it takes to channel your enthusiasm into a private conversation with one of your closest friends. That's the kind of emergency cell phones are really meant to handle!

How high should a parent set the bar? My wife would be happy if our son has a "good time" with music. I am hoping for something more. How can I explain to her the difference between a good musician and a great one?

This difference between good and great is a matter of personal opinion, so here's mine. Good musicians play their instruments with accuracy, tone, and feeling. These come with study, time, and effort. Most good musicians—not all—read music well. Some, but not all good musicians are comfortable improvising. They can pick up an instrument and make their way through unfamiliar songs at a party. Good musicians can play cooperatively with other musicians in an ensemble or band. Some do well accompanying singers with subtlety and feeling.

A great musician plays and reads music well, improvises, communicates intuitively with other musicians in an ensemble setting, and interprets music with his or her own, unique voice. She has confidence in her knowledge of music theory. It allows her to play with musical forms and change them to express her mood or point of view. Her intimate knowledge of the music and her instrument sets her apart from other players. Her instrumental tone, the power she exercises over dynamics, and her ability to play and interact creatively—these are the accomplishments of someone who can make music both inside and outside the box.

Some extraordinary musicians take our breath away in just a few soul-piercing notes. Think of musicians whose signature sounds you can identify after hearing just the opening notes of a recording, and you'll get my point. B.B. King. Johnny Cash. Eric Clapton. Miles Davis. Leo Kottke. Luciano Pavarotti. Itzhak Perlman. Jean-Pierre Rampal. Richard Thompson. Each one has developed a sound and style unlike any other.

Great musicians demonstrate qualities such as curiosity, ingenuity, creative thinking and problem solving, inner drive, and a courageous spirit that calls for taking musical risks. But these qualities alone, while highly admirable, do not make a fully realized musician. Some musical skills, such as reading music or instrumental technique, must be acquired inside the box. These take hard work, focus, and endless practice. Great

Great musicians demonstrate qualities such as curiosity, ingenuity, creative thinking and problem solving, inner drive, and a courageous spirit that calls for taking musical risks.

Open-ended questions ask kids to imagine the possibilities, describe their dreams, invent unlikely solutions, create new language to express their unique points of view. When this process of free thinking translates into music, an artist emerges.

musicians exercise self-discipline and hold their own performances up to scrutiny. They know when they can do better, and they refuse to settle for less in their own playing. Great musicians drive themselves nuts sometimes, but it's all for art's sake. You have to be a little crazy to be great.

To help children develop the potential for musical greatness, we must first encourage them to master the language, rules, and structures of music as they already exist. If they also learn to play their instruments well, they'll become good musicians who can play inside the box. But great musicians go farther to explore all manner of musical expression.

One way we can help children learn to think and play outside the box is to engage them in conversations that begin with open-ended questions. These questions have no fixed or right answers. They beg for discussion. Open-ended questions ask kids to imagine the possibilities, describe their dreams, invent unlikely solutions, create new language to express their unique points of view. When this process of free thinking translates into music, an artist emerges.

Some open-ended questions contain "if/then" or "how would you" premises. For example, if your son plays a passage of music in a predictable way or without much feeling, you might be tempted to tell him "jazz things up" or "put more feeling into it." Why not prompt him to unlock his imagination instead? The right open-ended question could put him in touch with some feelings about the music. His playing could improve naturally in an instant. You might ask him to play the piece as if he were telling you a funny or touching story. This will help him shift his perspective without telling him what you expect. You could ask him to play the piece as if he were one of the characters in a story or on a television show. Suddenly the music would become more flexible to him, more reflective of mood or personality.

Asking open-ended questions takes practice. This is especially true if you are used to simplifying things. Reducing questions into fact-finding equations with solitary "right" answers does eliminate confusion, but it also prevents creativity.

If you want to nurture artistic genius, you'll have to steer away from right/wrong, black-and-white answers. You'll need to take a genuine interest in what your child thinks and says. Asking questions in an open-ended fashion requires taking a trial-and-error approach. If one of your questions just makes him shrug, try asking it a different way. Eventually you'll come up with something that helps him take a fresh look at the music and how he's playing it. A few days of fumbling will make you a near expert on this process.

Reducing questions into fact-finding equations with solitary "right" answers does eliminate confusion, but it also prevents creativity.

Learning to nurture real creativity is well worth your effort. Studies show that the benefits of creativity far exceed the realm of music. Successful companies say they look for creativity in potential employees. Everyone from software designers to doctors do better work when they can look at situations a number of different ways. Creativity is best learned through the arts, but arts education is habitually cut whenever schools run short on money. So our children are taught to become convergent thinkers—that is, they learn the rules and live within the boundaries of what is acceptable. To us, this should be unacceptable.

Convergent thinking applies to everything from letter-sound combinations and the value of numbers to playground behavior. Starting in a traditional first-grade classroom, children are taught to memorize information. In second grade, they learn to take tests and pass them in order to prove themselves in school. Students who can think convergently may be able to predict what the teacher will ask of them. These students stand to fare the best. In third grade, students memorize the multiplication tables, complex spelling rules, and local historical facts. This kind of learning is often taught in a narrow, straightforward manner, although it need not be. Education should bring our children's minds, hearts, and souls to life rather than teaching them to settle for easy answers.

Some teachers are able to help children learn to think creatively. But the increasing pressure that principals and teachers feel to prepare students to succeed on standardized tests runs counter to providing them

If they are to develop original minds and voices, children must be encouraged to challenge the accepted wisdom, think for themselves, and express their thoughts and feelings in unique and unusual ways.

with instruction that promotes uniqueness and divergent thinking. So it takes an unusual parent or teacher to support a child to step out onto the road less traveled. But *that* road is the one that leads to artistic greatness.

If they are to develop original minds and voices, children must be encouraged to challenge the accepted wisdom, think for themselves, and express their thoughts and feelings in unique and unusual ways. And sometimes they also need someone to remind them to practice.

Chapter 17

All in the Musical Family

My son is studying oboe, and his tone is unavoidably dreadful. I'm ashamed to say that as painful as the practicing is for him, it might be worse for me. I can't stand listening when he plays scales. I want to encourage him, but lately I've begun asking him to practice behind closed doors. Can you offer any advice?

Only time and patience will lessen your pain and his. Oboe is tough. The truth is that, regardless of what instrument a child studies, almost every family endures months of honking, buzzing, or squeaking at the beginning. Some kids sound horrible for a long couple of years. Here are a few survival suggestions, offered with sympathy for you and yours.

- Gauge the level of your son's dedication to playing oboe before you close that door. If he feels secure in his choice and goals, he could be able to handle your distance. But shutting him away definitely communicates a negative message that could make a less confident child feel rejected. Tricky for you, and worth your consideration.

- Consider how your son might handle independent practice. Can he stay with his practice exercises and routines without having an adult present? If your goal is to help him achieve total independence with practice, perhaps you can help him learn to go solo one or two activities at a time; check in every five to ten minutes. Stick around for the last five. Fake a smile. That's love

- If those repetitive practice exercises are driving *you* nuts, image how *he* feels. Your child is learning patience, and so are you. Empathize.

- When his tone makes your houseplants wilt and the cat hide, take a long, deep breath and visualize a brighter future. If that fails, run somewhere out of sight as fast as you can and shout into a pillow. Also move the plants and let the cat go outside. Commend his perseverance.

- When your child feels down about his sound, encourage a positive attitude but sympathize with his suffering. Tell him about something important you've done that took real fortitude and patience. Show him a movie about a real-life hero. Make comparisons.

- Praise your child's efforts. Compliment whatever small improvements you notice. Look for increments of progress in the details: better finger positions, breathing, posture, energy, speed between changing notes. The more you cheer, the faster his sound will improve.

- Be stoic. Remember those sleep-deprived years. This is much easier than cooking breakfast after waking up with him four times during the night. It beats eleven diaper changes a day.

- Help your child develop a whopping good sense of humor. Memorize bad music jokes and tell them to him when he is most down. (What do you call a perfect pitch? When you land a banjo and an accordion into the dumpster on the first try.)

- Show him *Tackling the Monster*, a Sony video featuring Wynton Marsalis and Yo-Yo Ma. These inspirational musicians tell it like it is and offer kids great advice about how to make practice sessions more productive. Kids will find these teachers likeable, funny, and honest.

- As difficult as learning to play the oboe is, the experience may help your son develop what psychologists call frustration tolerance. (Others call it character building. I wonder whose it builds more— yours or his?) Remember this when he says he feels like quitting.

Frustration tolerance is an essential life skill that enables people to deal well with prolonged, challenging tasks and situations. Developing it during childhood is exceptionally valuable. Children can acquire frustration tolerance gradually, through repeated exposure to challenges that can be overcome only with patience and ample practice. People who do not develop frustration tolerance in childhood start to look like big babies to everyone else when life gets tough. To succeed in any great endeavor, we need to be able to delay gaining satisfaction. Rome was not built in a day. But children always want things now.

So it goes that parents do not serve their children well by placating all their needs and making things easy throughout childhood. Sometimes we can do our kids more good by letting them wrestle their challenges to the ground. This is one reason music lessons are such fertile ground! Musical study provides students with an effective medium through which they can learn to delay gratification; they learn that sometimes they must settle for small triumphs and keep on pluggin'. So when his screeching makes you want to screech back, remember: Frustration tolerance is good. Frustration tolerance is good. Frustration tolerance *is* good.

My fourth-grader has terrible taste in music, and she blasts it in all of our ears. Even her grunge-loving older brother is annoyed. She walks around the house with her belly button on display, tossing her hair, and singing through her nose. She makes serious attempts to sound sexy (what's a dad to do?). Now she's begging for a belly-button ring. I'm feeling like this has gone far enough. Is there anything I can do to influence her taste in music or fashion, or should I ask my doctor for a sedative?

I'd recommend the sedative. Imitating pop divas is pretty normal for preteen girls. In some cases, the phase goes away all by itself—unless your daughter gets discovered by talent scouts and signs a recording deal. But one stroll around the local mall will convince you that her behavior and taste in music are 100 percent normal. She is a product of her culture. Maybe you can find something cute about it all as a way to cope. Good luck.

While this midriff-diva thing lasts, it sounds as though you are going to feel better if you set limits or start working the 3-to-11 shift. You do have the right to voice your opinions and ask your daughter to keep her self expression within reasonable limits while she is around you. This means exercising some parental rights that may result in some door slamming, name calling, and brooding—predictable adolescent responses to parental criticism.

It's not about the music, Dad. It's about her identity and her generation.

You want to pass aesthetic values onto a young person who feels that her personal integrity requires her to be different than you.

But there's one thing I can tell you: It's not about the music, Dad. It's about her identity and her generation.

Some people's parents hated Elvis. Some hated the Beatles. Some shrugged or winced at the groaning of Leonard Cohen or the sneering rasp of Bob Dylan. It may be unfair to compare those groundbreaking artists with glossy pop icons like Shakira, but as agents of pop-culture change, their roles aren't much different. The beat goes on, even if you don't like it as much.

You can try to express your feelings in a neutral voice so as not to incur a new fight. But she'll likely get your message and hate it. You can set and enforce a dress code, put a volume limit on your daughter's CD player, take the television out of her room, and say "no" to requests to attend certain parties. Suppressing your daughter's modern taste may make your home more livable in some ways, but it could make it less livable in others. The only way out now is in.

You wish to positively influence her taste in music. This is probably not the easiest time to try, but it's worth making the effort. You want to pass aesthetic values onto a young person who feels that her personal integrity requires her to be different than you. So you'll have to align yourself with her point of view first. Otherwise you'll go into direct competition for her loyalties with social norms and her friends' attitudes.

To win your daughter's trust, you will have to meet her on her side of the line. At all costs, avoid discussions in which her choice of artists is pitted against your own. You'll have to be open to her musical preferences. That means really *listening* to her music. The best any parent can do under these conditions is to relax and have fun with the process. (And complain to your friends in private later.)

As for helping your daughter develop a more natural singing voice, this is a matter of stealthy maneuvering and tact. She might like her unnatural sound. You could offer to record her and let her listen back. If she doesn't *like* what she hears, you can bet she'll change it. That's the perfect moment to offer voice lessons. (If she likes the sound of her voice, well, then you'll be hearing even more of it.) You might also play CDs of indisputably great female vocalists while she's around the house. This way she can listen without actually meaning to.

If you can meet your daughter halfway, maybe she'll return the courtesy and listen to recordings of singers whose voices you enjoy. No telling what might expand her horizons.

Here are a few mind-expanding activities that might appeal to your grade school diva.

- Go music shopping together. Used CD shops are great for this. Buy two selections, one of her choosing, one of yours. Pick CDs you've been wanting, or try something experimental for both of you. Then have a listening party. Read the liner notes. After you hear each CD, share what you both liked and disliked. If you accept each other's opinions as valid, the discussion could foster musical understanding. Doing this from time to time will keep a fresh musical dialogue open between you.

- Have a deejay night. Ask your child to be the lead deejay and tell you all about her music. She can play you her favorite selections. Keep an open mind, no matter what, and do not disparage her taste, *even if you do not like the music.* Be kind. You'll get your chance to be the guest deejay. When you play her one or two favorite cuts, share your insights about them. When she insults them, ask for the same respect from her that she is receiving from you!

- Since kids like hearing stories about their parents when they were younger, you might play her music you listened to when you were her age. Tell her what life was like when you first heard that music. Kids like to know what you wore, what cars you drove, how you behaved, what dances were in, and the popular slang of the day. Reminiscing might bring you closer.

- Rent musical films to watch together on cold or rainy days. Anything from *Singin' in the Rain, The Music Man,* and *West Side Story* to *Grease* will provide family fun and a couple hours of classic music. Remember the popcorn.

We have three kids, each spaced about two and a half years apart from the next. They can be very loving with each other but also tend to act competitive. We have limited financial resources but would like to provide music lessons for all of them. Can you please suggest some approach to getting all three children involved in lessons? Of course, we want to avoid stirring up any unnecessary sibling rivalry.

This one is a tough nut to crack. The last thing you'll want to do is have the children draw straws, then give lessons to one child only. That strategy could lead to all-out war! Keeping in mind your goals of fair and equal participation as well as financial feasibility, let's consider these options:

- Look into music classes through the local recreation center if you have one. These tend to be more affordable than private lessons.

- Investigate whether the children's school offers any low-cost extra-curricular music programs during or after school. Some schools have before- or after-school choir, band, or guitar programs. Public schools usually offer these activities for little or no charge.

- If you can encourage your children to share a musical focus (perhaps just for now), look for a music teacher who will give them lessons as a group. Perhaps an all-family vocal lesson or strings lesson, taught ensemble-style, would work. Guitar is easily taught to four people at a time, so you could join the fun, too.

- Some music teachers might reduce your fee if all three children are studying. Inquire whether some sort of financial accommodation might be possible.

- If you are interested in obtaining scholarship money to help fund music lessons, contact the local chapters of music education organizations and music educators' associations to inquire whether any scholarships will be available in the coming year. These same institutions may also be able to help you locate qualified member teachers who agree to see a few students each year on a sliding-scale basis. It doesn't hurt to ask. To find the national contact information for such organizations, please read "Resources."

As for keeping the peace, I strongly recommend you make your expectations for the children clear from the start. Set the bar high for their considerate treatment of one another. (Assume the worst, then prevent it.) Present the children with a set of consequences that will ensue if they break the peace with each other. A logical consequence for rudeness might involve losing the privilege of attending the family lesson that week.

After laying some ground rules, how about promoting a vision? Get your kids thinking about their potential to make music together. There's no question that musical families have special musical advantages. People who are lucky enough to grow up singing close harmonies and playing in a family band are bound to sound great and lead musical lives. Perhaps your children need to hear some examples of successful musical families. The Carters, first family of hillbilly and country music, wrote and performed many beloved songs now considered classics. First came A.P. Carter, his wife, Sara, and their daughter, Janette. When A.P. passed away, Janette and her aunt Maybelle formed the group Mother Maybelle and the Carter Sisters. They recorded together and joined the Grand Ole Opry. Maybelle's daughter, June Carter, married Johnny Cash, and together they helped shape country music. Today, their daughter Roseanne Cash carries on the family legacy as a sensitive, literate songwriter. Elizabeth Von Trapp, granddaughter of the Von Trapp family (portrayed in *The Sound of Music*) is touring today.

There are so many more famous examples of musical families, such as the Jackson Five, the Carpenters, the Neville Brothers, and the Marsalis family. The currently popular trio Nickel Creek features brother and sister Sean and Sarah Watkins along with mandolin marvel Chris Thile. These three began playing together when they were barely old enough to tie their shoes, and they were nurtured and joined in making music by Chris' bass-player dad, Scott.

> *There's no question that musical families have special musical advantages. People who are lucky enough to grow up singing close harmonies and playing in a family band are bound to sound great and lead musical lives.*

If you introduce your children to this model of family music-making, you might be able to short-circuit sibling rivalry and keep your kids enjoying each other and working toward a common goal.

Here are a few things you can do to promote family harmony while your children take music lessons concurrently or are studying as a group:

- Organize regular family music nights where you all play and sing together. Arrange songs so each person has a part. Emphasize the value of supportive playing.

- Allow each child to choose a song for the family to learn and play together.

- Let each child have a turn being the featured soloist.

- Have a zero-tolerance policy for rude commentary. Do not permit your children to say anything disparaging about each other's musical abilities or efforts. Keep humor friendly.

- If the kids have been competing at home or you think one of them is feeling insecure, let their music teacher know. Give extra support.

- From time to time, arrange for each sibling to have a little private time with the music instructor.

- Ask the teacher to be careful not to encourage sibling rivalry by making comparisons.

- Encourage your children to explore different musical styles. This will broaden all of their musical horizons while allowing them to individuate from one another.

- Establish a code of respect in the family that applies to recitals or concerts. When one child is performing, ask the others to attend the event, and follow up with a family celebration afterward. This fosters your children's pride in each other and also gives each non-performing child a sense that his day will also come.

- If and when one sibling receives more public recognition than the others for musical talents, do not focus solely on that child. Resist the temptation to brag about him/her in front of your other kids.

The less-recognized siblings need your support even more at these times to avoid feeling inferior. Allow them to talk openly without fear of recrimination about feeling jealous; assure them that their time in the spotlight will come. Do all this without short-changing your spotlit child from her fifteen minutes of glory—and if you succeed, pass go and collect $200.

My nephew is a highly accomplished young pianist at seven. His teacher and his dad (my brother) are always pushing him to enter and win competitions. His mother is completely engrossed in his "brilliant career." Sad to say, he has no real buddies. He seems uncomfortable around others, rigid, and quiet. I look at him and wonder if he's getting any joy out of this. Sure, he likes to play piano, but it doesn't seem like enough. I just wish my brother and sister-in-law would help him develop a more normal social life. Is there anything I can say to convince them to ease up? It doesn't seem healthy for such a little guy to be so anxious.

Your concern is very valuable. You want to know that your nephew isn't going to crack up by age 20. The 1996 film *Shine* (directed by Scott Hicks) tells the dramatic story of pianist David Helfgott, a former child prodigy who was pushed too hard to make the most of his musical abilities. Although his story is extreme, the film shows us how too much pressure to succeed can harm a person's mental health.

Clearly, you'd like to see your nephew find happiness, friendship, and balance. It sounds as though your brother and sister-in-law are trying to fulfill their own desires to feel important and special through their son's accomplishments. I sense that your nephew's piano teacher is complicit in this dynamic, too. Managing a prodigy is tricky business.

Your nephew's talent has made him special but also set him up to be a victim of his success as well as the demands of his needy parents. This is always tragic for children. They learn early on to sacrifice their own needs and feelings in order to placate their parents. They may become unconsciously bound to unhealthy relationships, continuing to give what should not be asked of children in exchange for some desperately needed acceptance and nurturing. One step out of line and children in this position fear that their parent will withhold affection or lash out. To the outside world, the parents of gifted and seemingly compliant may seem charming. But behind closed doors, their children may be seeing something very different. Alice Miller's book titled *The Drama of the Gifted Child: The Search for the True Self* (HarperCollins) addresses this problem with clarity and power. Perhaps by reading it, you will acquire helpful insights into your nephew's situation.

The question remains what to do. It's entirely possible that your relatives would not hear a word you said if you directly voiced your concern. They would take your comment as a personal affront and rebuke you. Perhaps this is why you've hesitated. Narcissistic people are emotionally fragile, needy, and very easily hurt. They tend to become openly hostile toward anyone who poses a threat. If this describes your brother and his wife, you might try to find an indirect approach to giving support to your nephew.

You can probably do the greatest amount of good at this time by getting more actively but informally involved in his life. Attend his recitals and all, but do much more to get him into the world. Suggest music-related activities you can do with him that your brother and sister-in-law will interpret as nonthreatening. Take him to dinner where a jazz ensemble is playing. Take him to a ball game, to hear the national anthem and have fun. Invite him to a musical. Any excuse you can think of to get him away from the world of practice and perfection should feel like a great relief. Show him that you are someone who likes him for himself, not for his talent. Hang out and let musical activities be an acceptable excuse.

As he gets older, it's inevitable that your nephew will begin to explore the conflicts he feels regarding his parents and his music. You'll most likely be the first one he comes to when he's ready to talk. He'll know he can count on you to listen and help him work things through. This is really when you'll know how much your love and concern have made a difference. Good luck. Maybe with you in his life he will learn to let go and enjoy himself as his talent flourishes.

This is going to sound silly, but Grandpa is a little too enthusiastic about our son's musical accomplishments. Every time our son goes to visit him at his retirement villa, he chides him into performing. It's pretty embarrassing, but my dad just won't take no for an answer. Our son really hates this ritual and has started asking us to visit Grandpa without him. Could you suggest anything tactful we can do to turn this around?

Grandpa might be feeling bored or lonely these days. Seeing your son and having a special event to talk to his neighbors about may be the brightest spots in his life. He might even think that these little shows are a way of encouraging your boy to keep playing, and he may have no clue that they are damaging their relationship.

It sounds as if your dad would appreciate having more music, more activity, and more social time in his life. He needs a way to feel excited that keeps your son out of the hot seat. The activities coordinator and the geriatric social worker at your father's retirement facility could be just the people to help you develop a plan to give Grandpa what he needs. You and your son could help in ways that do not include impromptu recitals. If your dad really loves music, how about getting him a nice listening system and some new recordings? If he wants to learn more about music, you could also treat him to an exhilarating audio course on great music from the Learning Company. Then he could participate in conversations with your son at a whole new level.

As for turning around the situation with your son, I'd recommend explaining your son's feelings to Grandpa in terms of shyness around people he doesn't know well. You might offer to make Grandpa a home video of his grandson performing all his favorite numbers. Then he'd be able to watch the apple of his eye anytime and share the video with his friends.

If, despite this variety of strategies, Grandpa persists in putting your boy on the spot, you'll just have to take control of the situation. Some people just can't take a hint. I'd recommend being very direct and setting limits with your father. Let him know that if he wants his grandson to visit, he must refrain from asking him to perform, period. The best choice should be obvious, but if it isn't, put your son's needs first. Your dad will eventually get over it.

Chapter 18

Big Kids' Dreams of Fame and Fortune

My daughter insists she wants to be a pop star someday (before she's 18). Her vocal talent is probably fair, her people skills are excellent, and her enthusiasm is downright infectious. If anyone can win people's hearts, she can. I just wish the media didn't turn little girls who can sing into sex objects. Is there anything I can do to protect her from the hype and guide her in a productive direction?

It's true that the recording industry is signing younger and younger girls to recording deals these days. These junior divas have learned to mimic the singing styles of more mature singers, and the record-buying population falls in line. Sounds like your daughter is very musical and ambitious.

The lure of fame can provide kids with a mental diversion from reality of wearing braces, hating one's clothes, worrying about one's bust size, and trying to figure out who one's friends are during those typically awkward, insecure years. Who hasn't fantasized about being a star?

In addition to taking voice lessons, it sounds like your daughter might enjoy getting some training in modern dance—jazz and hip-hop to start—if she wants to follow in the footsteps of other young pop divas. Both activities would help her develop and assess her potential without limiting her musical style. Just as important, dance could build her self-confidence and put her in touch with other creative youth. Keeping her constructively engaged and growing in the direction of her dreams are appropriate goals right now.

Qualified teachers may also be able to help your daughter plan her first career moves, shoring up her drive and commitment. After high school, she might continue her training at Berklee College of Music in Boston or Musicians Institute in Hollywood. These schools prepare young people for professional careers in the music industry. You can help your daughter by researching her options with her and giving her your vote of confidence.

Pop-star dreams may come true for people who have vision, talent, a fiery determination to succeed, physical appeal, excellent luck, brilliant timing, or several of the above. If your daughter sticks with lessons, learns to audition and perform, and forms and follows a realistic plan of action, perhaps she'll be able to make her dream come true. If not, she'll have gained very valuable training, experience in the arts, life skills, and made some remarkable friends. These she will keep even if she moves on. She stands a better chance of succeeding with you behind her. More important, she will survive whatever disappointments come her way knowing you love and support her, regardless.

Performing often serves as a gateway to other careers in the arts. If your daughter's dream of fame and fortune loses its spark, she might consider getting involved with other aspects of the music business. There are so many other related careers to consider. Since she's good with people, she would probably have fun working in public relations or artist management. This kind of work typically takes place in Los Angeles and New York. PR agents and record company executives enjoy exciting lifestyles. Your daughter might learn to personally assist artists, coordinate or manage concert tours, or handle promotion. Within the recording industry, each company also employs talent scouts and people who help develop and supervise artists and their recording careers.

Then there are technical careers in music. Great math skills combined with an analytic mind and the love of music could predispose her to being an excellent business manager, handling the financial matters of a performer's career, or working in an administrative capacity for any of the businesses within the music industry.

Maybe she has a scientific bent. If she is fascinated by gizmos, dials, electronics, and computers, she could be very happy developing a career in the world of music recording. Audio engineering is both technical and artistic. This work fits the thinker, the private personality, the ana-lytic/artistic type who can exercise taste and ingenuity during the pro-duction of music. Recording engineers and producers work directly with performers and influence the sound of their recordings. If she's really crazy about weird science, she might even become a designer of new recording and sound equipment or a clinician who teaches recording engineers how to use their new gear. She could surprise you.

Let's also consider all that music-making for television, film, and radio. Each medium hires writers, reviewers, announcers, composers, and other people in front and in back of the cameras and mics. And every piece of music you hear has to be published by someone. There are a number of careers in music publishing that she might enjoy. Every music book and piece of sheet music passes through many stages, each one supervised by an individual with special training. Whether she makes deals between songwriters, artists, and publishers, clears copy-rights of songs for publications, actually transcribes or engraves the sheet music, or designs cover art, she would be actively involved with music-making and the music business.

You can see what a vast array of possibilities exists within the music industry. The Berklee College of Music offers wonderful training in music business careers as well as in performance, composition, and all the rest. If you invite her to visit the school's website, she'll see how people who really want to become professional musicians train for it, and what they can also learn to do along the way.

Your daughter has a lot to gain by exploring her potential in the music industry. Be her confidant, her rock, and her biggest fan. Remind her that her choices are vast and that her creative potential is without limits. She will always appreciate you for it. And when she gets stuck or disappointed every now and then, mail her a ticket back home.

Our teenage son has been playing guitar in a rock band since his last year in ele-mentary school. He's talking about deferring college and moving to L.A. to see if he can make it as a musician. He's good and he's responsible, but it seems like guitar players are a dime a dozen. Should we be counseling him against this plan?

Your son has been practicing, playing, and working in an ensemble for many years already. He is clearly a dedicated musician. Sure, there are a lot of good guitar players, but there's always room for someone

You do not have to support the L.A. star-making myth in order to support your son's dreams.

talented *and* responsible. If he is a quick study, has a flair for performance, or has his own style, chances are that he will get opportunities to audition and work.

Moving to L.A. and putting his nose into the music industry will teach your son a lot about himself and about people, and of course he'll find out how the music business works. He has youth and ambition on his side. It could take him years to succeed there, so it's best to be practical. This will probably not be a one-year proposition.

L.A. is home to the entire entertainment industry. So in addition to working in bands, many musicians play their instruments in the recording studios. Music of all kinds for television, film, and interactive media is always being composed and recorded. With the right connections, your son could become a successful session player. We do not often see these players' faces on T.V., but they are among the finest in the world at what they do.

Some musicians discover that they enjoy the technical side of recording—engineering, producing, and mixing music. Players can learn these skills through specialized training and practical experience in the studios. The Full Sail School of Real World Education in Winterland, Florida, for instance, offers college-level training in the recording arts. This kind of program could allow your son to add engineering to his list of employable musical skills.

You do not have to support the L.A. star-making myth in order to support your son's dreams. As a parent, you have the power to help him understand that he will be able to have a rich musical life and a successful career no matter where he lives—even if he does not turn into a Hollywood sensation. Encouragement to explore his chosen path with a backup plan in mind is what he needs from you now. He'll feel OK about coming home or relocating if he changes his mind and his dream.

Becoming a hometown success story is pretty rewarding in and of itself. Musicians who structure local careers correctly are able to earn a living playing music without eating road food. Indeed, a lot of bands hit the *Billboard* charts without ever having lived in Los Angeles or New York. They make a name for themselves at home, and word travels.

The lifestyle of a bread-and-butter musician is more hand-to-mouth than other kinds of employment. But steady work is always available for competent musicians. Think of all the dance bands, wedding bands, and local ensembles we like to listen to. The best ones are booked for parties many months in advance. Those musicians enjoy their work and are paid well to do what they love.

A general business musician can integrate all kinds of work into a multifaceted career.

A general business musician can integrate all kinds of work into a multifaceted career. One day in the studio, another teaching private students, and another day working on composition or production for a radio ad. Many musicians double as accompanists, rehearsal pianists, choir directors, and music specialists in the schools. Some with an artistic vision record their own CDs, selling them locally and over the Internet.

I wouldn't let the rock-star dream worry you too much. During youth, aiming high is a sign of self-confidence and vision. It only gets risky when a young person keeps dreaming to the exclusion of developing other employable skills. You'd be wise to help him avoid locking himself into a narrow concept of musical success.

Some musicians increase their odds for success by taking courses or earning degrees in business. For example, even though he had been discovered as a child prodigy in India and was later chosen to become the chief protégé of sitarist Ravi Shankar, Khartik Seshadri chose to study business and earn a degree. Today that training helps him successfully navigate through the deep waters of the international music scene. He travels and performs many months out of the year, sharing his rare talent and exquisite music with thousands of appreciative fans.

Business knowledge helps the performing artist deal with contracts, managers, agents, publishers, producers, promoters, and attorneys. The University of Southern California School of Cinema and Television offers a special certificate in entertainment business for MBA students, with courses in entertainment marketing, entertainment finance, and so on. Your son could someday live in L.A., study at USC, and take the music business by storm! (This idea could provide some added incentive now to get his homework in on time and study for tests.)

Yes, it's a jungle out there. I hope you will encourage your son to practice swinging from tree to tree. If he can view himself and his creativity in positive, realistic terms, he should be well-equipped to pursue his youthful ambitions and live a fully musical life. What more could any parent hope for?

Resources

In this section you will find a basic list of recordings, books, websites, organizations, and other resources that relate to the topics discussed in this book. You can find out more about each listed resource with a quick Internet search that includes a title or keyword plus any other information you have, such as an author or recording artist name. The list is by no means comprehensive, but it provides some excellent places to start for anyone interested in becoming more informed.

Recordings

Quiet time recordings = QT. Activity time recordings = AT.

Infants and Toddlers

Joanie Bartels, *Put on Your Dancing Shoes*, BMG Special Products. Upbeat world-music dance tunes with Bartels's infectious voice. Great for high-energy times and parties. AT

Heidi Brende, *SmartPlay with Classical*, the Orchard. Lively, happy classical piano selections played in their original forms to accompany young children's playtimes. Listen for Prokofiev's "Music for Children," Schumann's "Scenes from Childhood," and "Four Little Pieces," which Mozart composed at the age of eight. AT

Allison DeSalvo, *Happiness Is All Around You*, World of Song. Joyful, energetic, and dramatic, DeSalvo's style will spark children's innate musicality, self-expression, and imagination while encouraging families to interact in meaningful and playful ways. AT

Joel Frankel, *JoJo the Scarecrow*, Waterdog Music. This recording offers the best wordplay children's music has to offer. These catchy songs about creatures both great and small and Frankel's friendly musical style get children excited about singing and rhyming. AT

Jessica Harper, *40 Winks*, Alacazam. Harper's imaginative lyrics, top-notch musicianship, and mellow, rich vocals will help parents and children wind down together. QT

Fred Koch, *This Lil' Cow*, Red Rover. Koch's fun, friendly style welcomes young listeners to make music with him through sing-alongs, movement games, and listening activities. AT

Sherry Goffin Kondor, *Mellow My Baby*, Rounder. Thirteen gentle songs followed by instrumental tracks so baby can hear you sing. Soothing and exceptionally musical. QT

Bob McGrath, *Sing Me a Story*, BMI. Thirteen original songs sung by McGrath (of *Sesame Street*) and played by some of the greatest studio musicians in New York. Top-rate musicianship and loads of fun with a familiar friend from TV. AT

Steve Rashid, *I Will Hold Your Tiny Hand*, Woodside Avenue Music. Subtitled "Evening Songs and Lullabies," this stellar collection features Rashid's gentle voice and outstanding musical production. QT

Kathy Reid-Naiman, *Say Hello to the Morning*, Merriweather. A delightful collection of children's songs, rhymes, and singing games that makes singing and playing along very easy. Both an excellent teaching tool and fun to share at home. AT

Joanne Shenandoah, *All Spirits Sing*, Music for Little People. A collection of pretty, soothing songs by a deeply melodic singer who expresses her love of her Iroquois culture through music. QT

Bill Staines, *The Happy Wanderer*, Folk Legacy. Songwriter of the beloved "A Place in the Choir," Staines has a warm, folky voice that wends it way through traditional and original songs young children will love. AT

Various artists, *The Celtic Lullaby*, Ellipsis Arts. A host of Celtic artists who are beloved in the British Isles and North America appear on this gorgeous collection of lullabies. QT

Various artists, *Daddies Sing Good Night*, Sugar Hill. Dads, all of them well-known folk and bluegrass artists, sing children to sleep with a wonderful selection of songs. QT

Various artists, *On a Starry Night*, Windham Hill. Tracy Silverman, producer and former violinist with the Turtle Island String Quartet, is joined by Bobby McFerrin, jazzer Billy Taylor, Airto and Flora Purim, Keola Beamer, Nightnoise, and pianists Jim Brickman and George Winston. Passionate and gentle, good music for young ears. QT

Ages Two to Seven

Peter and Ellen Allard, *Sing It, Say It, Stamp It, Sway It*, Vols. 1, 2, and 3, 80-Z Music. Three CDs of original and traditional songs, finger plays, circle games, cumulative songs, echo chants, and silly rhymes. Folky, straightforward, active, and cheerful. AT

Linda Arnold, *Happiness Cake*, Youngheart. Linda Arnold's crystalline voice and magic-infused songs have the power to sweep children into a land of make-believe where fantastic characters make discoveries and friends. This CD contains rich musical production and Arnold's strongest original material, with unforgettable songs like "There's a Dinosaur Knocking at My Door." AT

The Banana Slug String Band, *Goin' Wild!* Slug Music. The Banana Slugs blend acoustic and electric instruments with their animated vocal style to create lively music all about animals, nature, and science. This particular CD focuses on the wildlife in Yellowstone and the Tetons. High energy, great content, catchy tunes. AT

Tim Cain, *Tim for the Kids*, Tim's Tunes. This gentle-voiced singer-songwriter, formerly of Sons of Champlin, gives very young children songs to sing about the wonders of nature, accompanied by very pretty instrumentation. On one side of the cassette, Cain sings. On the other, children can take the lead. Great for nurturing musicality! QT

Donovan, *Pied Piper*, Music for Little People. He always had that child-like charm and still does. This collection includes "I Love My Shirt," "Happiness Runs," and others, as well as some newer compositions performed by the master and his grandchildren. AT

Norman Foote, *One Thousand Pennies*, Shoebox Music. The Canadian singer combines calm moments with silly ones in a recording that integrates guitar, accordion, pennywhistle, percussion, harmonica, and mandolin, with the sound of dropping pennies on the title track. QT

Judy Caplan Ginsburgh, *Sing Along and Smile*, Judy Music. A delightful mix of children's songs that promote learning, self-esteem, and values. AT

The Happy Crowd, *Gettin' Happy*, Big Smile Entertainment. This band elevates kids' music in the pop-rock style to something adults can enjoy, too. Clever songs on subjects as relevant and diverse as thoroughly brushing your teeth and understanding ecology are interspersed with funny songs and sweet numbers about friendship. Perfect for rockers in preschool through kindergarten. AT

Tish Hinojosa, *Cada Niño, Every Child*, Rounder. A charming collection of songs by this notable singer-songwriter, with every number performed in both Spanish and English (printed lyrics included). The CD rolls along through a variety of moods and subjects, interweaving songs and stories to acoustic accompaniment. This is musical multiculturalism at its best. AT

Ella Jenkins, *Ella Jenkins and a Union of Friends Pulling Together,* Smithsonian Folkways. The roots and essence of folk music for children. Jenkins reaches children in preschool, kindergarten, and primary school through a variety of songs, rhymes, and stories with her message of love, family, and community. AT

John Lithgow, *Singin' in the Bathtub,* Sony. Swing jazz, wacky lyrics filled with wordplay, a 30-piece band, and the humor of John Lithgow rolled into one CD. Too much fun! AT

Ric Louchard, *Ragtime Romp,* Music for Little People. An evenly paced presentation of some of Scott Joplin's most loved compositions alongside others that are lesser known. An instrumental album that lends itself to quiet play, this is a great introduction to the world of ragtime. AT

Taj Mahal, *Shake Sugaree,* Music for Little People. Taj Mahal, master storyteller and folk-blues legend, offers this tapestry of songs and informal introductions for young listeners. The CD includes blues songs and bluesy numbers such as the title track by Elizabeth Cotten and the ever-popular "Fishing Blues." Essential roots listening for fresh ears. AT

Ladysmith Black Mambazo, *Gift of the Tortoise,* Music for Little People. Gorgeous a cappella renditions of Zulu songs and stories interwoven. A lovely way to introduce children to the sounds of South Africa. AT

John McCutcheon, *Mail Myself to You,* Rounder. An essential, classic children's album combining McCutcheon's folksy style and excellent musicianship on hammered dulcimer, fiddle, mandolin, banjo, guitars, and piano. A sure winner for the songs, topics, and talent. AT

Sally Rogers, *Piggyback Planet,* the Orchard. Singable ecologically minded songs with a range of musical styles and Rogers's bright, clear voice accompanied by acoustic instruments. AT

Pete Seeger, *American Folk, Game, and Activity Songs,* Smithsonian Folkways. Combining two prior recordings by the folk music pioneer, this recording features Seeger and his banjo at their most exuberant, getting everyone to sing, dance, and play along. AT

Various artists, *Latin Playground,* Putumayo World Music. This lively introduction to Latin American culture includes 11 songs performed in Spanish, English, Maya, or Portuguese by North, Central, and South American musicians. Song lyrics and liner notes in English and Spanish are included. AT

Grade Two and Above

Tom Chapin, *Around the World and Back Again,* Sony Wonder. A great introduction to Tom Chapin. The lyrical details of life around the world combined with Chapin's guitar, banjo, and wonderful voice make this a winner. AT

Martin Cookson, *Nottingham Fair,* Camsco. This recording portrays life during the English Renaissance as lived by a child. Narration interspersed with marvelously performed songs and tunes from the 1590s. AT

Daddy A Go Go, *Monkey in the Middle,* Boyd's Tone. Original rock 'n' roll tunes sporting retro and surf guitar and kid-friendly themes and lyrics. Good musical material for every age. AT

Jerry Garcia and David Grisman, *Not for Kids Only,* Acoustic Disc. The late Grateful Dead guitarist Jerry Garcia joined friend and mandolin wizard David Grisman in 1993 to make this recording, blending their talents and styles into a set of traditional tunes infused with humor. Kids and grown-ups are treated to twangy and jingly strings, rumbly singing voices, and nuances of bluegrass, swing, klezmer, and more. Fun wordplay and unique sounds that entice kids to sing and play along. AT

Bill Harley, *Down in the Backpack*, Round River Music. Bill Harley's humorous music and storytelling have been entertaining older kids and adults for years. This album is one of many worth hearing. AT

Lead Belly, *Lead Belly Sings for Children*, Smithsonian Folkways. Essential Lead Belly music including work songs and blues, nonsense, secular, and religious songs. Spoken introductions familiarize children with the great singer and songwriter as well as his material. AT

Richard Perlmutter, *Beethoven's Wig*, Rounder Kids. This recording familiarizes young listeners with famous classical pieces while turning the compositions into hilarious discourses on the composers and the times in which they lived. Instrumental versions at the end of the CD restore the pieces to their original integrity. Serious classical musicians may object, but children in elementary grades go crazy over the recording. AT

Rick Scott, *Philharmonic Fool*, Festival. If Robin Williams were a children's musical artist, he would be Rick Scott. Humor, compassion, insight, and absurdly musical (electric!) dulcimer playing make this a standout among Scott's recordings. AT

Sweet Honey in the Rock, *All for Freedom* and *Still the Same Me*, Music for Little People. High-spirited, intuitive, and powerful, this all-woman vocal ensemble interprets traditional and contemporary songs that celebrate the human condition, unity, and diversity. *Still the Same Me* also includes rhythm slams that start young musicians on the path of jamming and improvising together. AT

They Might Be Giants, *No!* Rounder. Literary pop-rock from a band grown-ups loved first. Interactive CD lets children tune in and participate on the computer as well. AT

Trout Fishing in America, *InFINity*, Trout. Off-the-chart funny and engaging, this collection of Trout Fishing musical romps will keep any self-respecting kid in stitches. Tongue-twisting lyrics, fast-paced music, expert musicianship, and a wacky sense of humor make this a great recording. AT

Various artists, *Circle Game*, Music for Little People. The young singers and beautiful production bring new emotional range and depth to well-known pop-folk hits from the '70s, including "The Hammer Song," "Moonshadow," and other musical treasures. QT

Various artists, *Reading Rainbow's Greatest Hits*, Oasis Music. Including the voices of Bobby McFerrin and Phoebe Snow, these songs from *Reading Rainbow* television shows cover a wide variety of interesting topics. AT

Organizations

Music Education and Therapy

American Music Therapy Association, 8455 Colesville Rd., Suite 1000, Silver Spring, MD 20910; (301) 589-3300; fax (301) 589-5175; www.musictherapy.org. The mission of AMTA is to advance public awareness of the benefits of music therapy and increase access to quality music therapy services in a rapidly changing world. AMTA can help you locate a music therapist.

American Orff-Schulwerk Association, PO Box 391089, Cleveland, OH 44139-8089; (440) 543-5366; www.aosa.org. The American Orff-Schulwerk Association is a professional organization of music and movement educators dedicated to the creative teaching approach developed by Carl Orff and Gunild Keetman. It is founded on the belief that learning about music—learning to sing and play, to hear and understand, to move and create—should be an active and joyful experience.

American String Teachers Association, 4153 Chain Bridge Rd., Fairfax, VA 22030; (703) 279-2113; fax (703) 279-2114; www.astaweb.com. ASTA is devoted to enhancing the future of string teaching and playing, and to strengthening this commitment and marshalling the resources needed to bring the joy of string playing and teaching to more children.

Bands of America, 39 W. Jackson Place, Indianapolis, IN 46225; (317) 636-2263; (800) 848-BAND; fax (317) 524-6200; www.bands.org. Founded in 1975, Bands of America is the nation's leading presenter of music events for high school band students.

Dalcroze Society of America, 272 Alleyne Dr., Cranberry Township, PA 16066-7402; www.dalcrozeusa.org. The Dalcroze Society of America is a nonprofit educational organization that welcomes musicians, dancers, actors, therapists, and artist-educators who study and promote the Dalcroze Eurhythmics approach to music learning through rhythmic movement, aural training, and improvisation.

The Gordon Institute for Music Learning, www.giml.org. The Gordon Institute offers specialized training in Dr. Edwin Gordon's Music Learning Theory and can be reached through the website. GIML publications are available from GIA Publications, 7404 South Mason Ave., Chicago, IL 60638; (800) GIA-1358; (708) 496-3800; fax (708) 496-3828; www.giamusic.com.

International Association for Jazz Education, PO Box 724, Manhattan, KS 66505; (785) 776-8744; fax (785) 776-6190; www.iaje.org. A voluntary nonprofit organization, IAJE initiates programs that nurture the understanding and appreciation of jazz and its heritage, provides leadership to educators regarding curriculum and performance, and assists teachers, students, and artists with information and resources.

International Foundation for Music Research, www.music-research.org. IFMR was founded in 1997 to support scientific research to explore the relationship between music and physical and emotional wellness, with particular attention to the impact of music making on at-risk youth. IFMR also convenes scientists, educators, and others around critical issues in music research and disseminates research through its publication, *IFMR News,* and various online research referral services and archives.

Mr. Holland's Opus Foundation, 15125 Ventura Blvd., Suite 204, Sherman Oaks, CA 91403; (818) 784-6787; fax (818) 784-6788; www.mhopus.org. Mr. Holland's Opus Foundation supports music education and its many benefits through the donation and repair of musical instruments to underserved schools, community music programs, and individual students nationwide.

Music Teachers National Association, 441 Vine St., Suite 505, Cincinnati, OH 45202-2811; (513) 421-1420; (888) 512-5278; fax (513) 421-2503; www.mtna.org. MTNA is committed to advancing the value of music study and music making to society and to supporting the professionalism of music teachers.

The National Association for Music Education (MENC), 1806 Robert Fulton Dr., Reston, VA 20191; (800) 336-3768; www.menc.org. The mission of MENC is to advance music education by encouraging the study and making of music by all.

National Band Association, (601) 297-8168; fax (601) 266-6185; www.nationalbandassoc.org. The National Band Association was organized for the purpose of promoting the musical and educational significance of bands and is dedicated to the attainment of excellence for bands and band music. NBA is open to anyone interested in bands, regardless of his/her experience, type of position held, or the specific level at which he/she works.

National Endowment for the Arts, 1100 Pennsylvania Ave. N.W., Washington, DC 20506; (202) 682-5400; www.nea.gov. The NEA serves the public good by nurturing the expression of human creativity, supporting the cultivation of community spirit, and fostering the recognition and appreciation of the excellence and diversity of our nation's artistic accomplishments.

National Foundation for Advancement in the Arts, 800 Brickell Ave., Suite 500, Miami, FL 33131; (305) 377-1140; fax (305) 377-1149; (800) 970-ARTS; www.nfaa.org. The NFAA's mission is to identify emerging artists and assist them at critical junctures in their educational and professional development, and to raise appreciation for, and support of, the arts in American society.

Organization of American Kodály Educators, 1612 29th Ave. S., Moorhead, MN 56560; (218) 227-6253; fax (218) 227-6254; www.oake.org. The mission of the OAKE is to enrich the quality of life of the people of the U.S.A. through music education by promoting the philosophy of Zoltán Kodály.

Percussive Arts Society, 701 N.W. Ferris Ave., Lawton, OK 73507-5442; (580) 353-1455; (800) 444-0507; fax (580) 353-1456; www.pas.org. PAS is a music service organization promoting percussion education, research, performance, and appreciation throughout the world.

The Tomatis Method, www.tomatis.com. The Tomatis Method is a program of sound stimulation, audio-vocal activities, and consultation using patented equipment. It focuses on how listening profoundly affects learning, speech/language, communication, thoughts, feelings, and relationships. Tomatis individuals improve their ability to listen, speak, sing, create, think, and learn. The Tomatis website lists addresses for centers in the U.S. and elsewhere.

Youth Education in the Arts, PO Box 506, Bergenfield, NJ 07621; www.yea.org. The mission of Youth Education in the Arts is to support the development of young people through participation in the performing arts. YEA provides programs that allow thousands of talented performers to participate in pageantry events around the continent. Included are the Cadets, the Crossmen Drum and Bugle Corps, and the U.S. Scholastic Marching Band Association.

Children's Music

The Children's Music Network, PO Box 1341, Evanston, IL 60204-1341; (847) 733-8003; www.cmnonline.org. Members of CMN meet and stay in touch to share songs and ideas about children's music, to inspire one another about the empowering ways adults and young people can communicate through music, and to be a positive catalyst for education and community-building through music. Their chapters work to support the creation and dissemination of life-affirming, multicultural musical forms for, by, and with young people. CMN regional chapters all around the country organize both local and regional gatherings that are open to CMN members and nonmembers alike.

Children's Music Web, www.childrensmusic.org. The Children's Music Web is a charitable activity of Pickleberry Pie that provides children and families with free online musical programming, recommendations for children's recordings, musical activities, and links to children's musical artists.

Music Instruction Programs

National Programs

Kindermusik International, 6204 Corporate Park Dr., Browns Summit, NC 27214; (800) 628-5687; (336) 273-3363; www.kindermusik.com. In a Kindermusik class, educators lead a group of parents and their children through joyful activities, using music and movement. Parents learn more about their child's unique developmental process, and the shared learning experience creates a unique bond as the child associates learning with fun musical play. The learning process continues at home, guided by specially designed books, CDs, and games.

Music for Young Children, 39 Leacock Way, Kanata, Ottawa, Ontario, K2K 1T1 Canada; (800) 561-1692; (613) 592-7565; fax (613) 592-9353; www.myc.com. The goal of MYC is to encourage children to develop "the happy habit of learning music." Over the course of the MYC year, a very young child's listening, vocal, and fine and gross motor skills develop and are refined. Musical concepts are taught at the child's learning level. Keyboard, singing, rhythm, theory, and composition are combined in each lesson to reinforce the teaching points of the lesson.

Music Together, 66 Witherspoon St., Princeton NJ 08542; (800) 728-2692; www.musictogether.com. Music Together is a music and movement approach to early childhood music development for infant, toddler, preschool, and kindergarten children and their parents, teachers, and other primary caregivers. The Music Together approach develops every child's birthright of basic music competence by encouraging the actual experiencing of music rather than the learning of concepts or information about music. Music Together CDs, songbooks, and classroom techniques enjoy widespread use by teachers and families.

Suzuki Association of the Americas, PO Box 17310, Boulder, CO 80308; (303) 444-0948; (800) 336-3768; www.suzukiassociation.org. The SAA is a coalition of teachers, parents, educators, and others who are interested in making music education available to all children. The SAA provides programs and services to members throughout North and South America. With the International Suzuki Association (ISA) and other regional associations, the SAA promotes and supports the spread of Dr. Suzuki's Talent Education.

Yamaha Music Education Course, www.yamaha.com/musiced. The Yamaha Music Education Course provides curricula for four- to eight-year-olds. The Junior Music Course for four- and five-year-olds is a two-year program that includes listening, singing, playing keyboard, and creating. The Young Musicians Course for six- to eight-year-old beginners is also a two-year program. Musicianship is taught through the use of the Yamaha Electone keyboard, capable of sounds ranging from the classical violin to the electric guitar. Children are involved in the following activities: singing, ear training, repertoire (keyboard pieces), ensemble playing (group performance), keyboard harmony, arranging, keyboard technique, sight singing, sight playing, and theory. The best way to locate a school that offers Yamaha instruction is to search online.

Professional Schools

Berklee College of Music, 1140 Boylston St., Boston, MA 02215-3695; (800) 237-5533; (617) 747-2221; www.berklee.edu.

Full Sail School of Real World Education, 330 University Blvd., Winter Park, Florida 32792, (800) 226-7625; www.fullsail.com. Offers a recordings arts program.

Musicians Institute, 1655 N. McCadden Place, Hollywood, CA 90028; (800) 255-7529; www.mi.edu.

The University of Southern California School of Cinema-Television, Los Angeles, CA 90089-2211; (213) 740-8358; www-cntv.usc.edu.

Summer Programs

Aspen Music Festival and School, 2 Music School Rd., Aspen, CO 81611; (970) 925-3254; fax (970) 925-5708; www.aspenmusicfestival.com. The Aspen Music Festival and School is a high-level training ground for the world's next generation of professional musicians. It offers programs from orchestra to opera, conducting to contemporary music, piano, guitar, and more; a student body ages eight to 68, from 39 countries and virtually every major conservatory; a distinguished faculty with experience in nearly every facet of music making; and 200-plus world-class concerts, master classes, and lectures, giving musicians the opportunity to deepen their musical skills over the summer months.

Blue Lake Fine Arts Camp, 300 East Crystal Lake Rd., Twin Lake, MI 49457; (800) 221-3796; fax (231) 893-5120; www.bluelake.org. Blue Lake Fine Arts Camp, a summer school of the arts located on a 1,300-acre campus in Michigan's Manistee National Forest, offers fine arts education for all ages. The summer camp annually serves over 4,500 gifted elementary, junior high, and high school students with diverse programs in music, art, dance, and drama while offering over 175 performances during its Summer Arts Festival. Blue Lake also operates a widely acclaimed International Exchange Program and two public radio stations. Instruction in the Suzuki method is featured along with choir and band programs.

Camp Ballibay for the Fine and Performing Arts, Box 1, Camptown, PA 18815; (570) 746-3223; fax (570) 746-3691; www.ballibay.com. Camp Ballibay offers a wide range of noncompetitive fine and performing arts activities in a traditional camp setting on a Pennsylvania mountaintop. Major activity areas include theater, vocal and instrumental music, ballet, modern, jazz and tap dance, video, radio, two- and three-dimensional visual arts, photography, and technical theater. The camp emphasizes individual choice in a noncompetitive program.

Camp Curtain Call, www.campcurtaincall.com. Summer: 849 River Rd., Dugspur, VA 24325; (276) 730-0233; fax (276) 730-0233. Winter: 7804 Sagefield Dr., Knoxville, TN 37920; (865) 573-7002; fax (865) 573-7002. Camp Curtain Call runs the musical gamut—any child can find an instrument to learn and an ensemble to join. Performance groups directed by professionals include concert band, pit orchestras, rock bands, chorus, and other ensembles. Private lessons are also available for most instruments.

Camp Encore-Coda, www.encore-coda.com. Summer: Stearns Pond, Sweden, ME 04040; (207) 647-3947. Winter: 32 Grassmere Rd., Brookline, MA 02467; (617) 325-1541. Since 1950 Camp Encore-Coda has welcomed spirited young people finishing grades three to 11 from all over the world, who love to make music, play sports, and enjoy good times in a Maine summer camp environment. The program includes chamber music, chorus, jazz bands, orchestras, rock bands and ensembles, and wind ensembles.

Cordova 4-H Bluegrass and Old Time Music and Dance Camp, Box 1053, Cordova, AK 99574; (907) 424-3943; fax (907) 424-3277. Campers ages nine to 18 learn bluegrass and old-time music. Specific services available for the physically challenged and visually impaired.

French Woods Festival of the Performing Arts, www.frenchwoods.com. Summer: PO Box 609, Hancock, NY 13783; (845) 887-5600; fax (845) 887-5075. Winter: PO Box 770100, Coral Springs, FL 33077-0100; (800) 634-1703; (954) 346-7455; fax (954) 346-7564. French Woods offers children from seven to 17 an opportunity to explore their interests and improve their abilities in a wide variety of performing and visual arts as well as more traditional camp activities. Each child is able to create a schedule that caters to his or her own interests and abilities.

Hidden Valley Camp, RR #1, Box 2360, Freedom, ME 04941; (207) 342-5177; fax (207) 342-5685; www.hiddenvalleycamp.com. Hidden Valley Camp offers a wide range of programs, including a pop/rock component that offers campers a chance to play guitar, drums, and percussion and sing in a rock band. The overall focus is on the creative and performing arts as well as horse care.

Idyllwild Arts Summer Program, PO Box 38, 52500 Temecula Drive, Idyllwild, CA 92549; (909) 659-2171; www.idyllwildarts.org. Students enrolled in the Idyllwild Arts Summer Program receive intensive, hands-on arts experience in a competition-free environment that emphasizes individual growth. The summer program consists of courses in dance, music, theater, visual arts, creative writing, and Native American arts. In the Children's Center (ages five to 12), the minimum boarding age is nine. In the Junior Artist's Center (ages 11 to 13), workshops include one- and two-week offerings in theater, visual arts, and creative writing. In addition, students in this age range may participate in selected Youth Arts Center music and dance courses based on experience and ability. A one-week Family Camp is also offered. Families live together and have the opportunity to explore the visual and performing arts in a relaxed setting. Adults and children choose from a variety of arts and outdoor activities. Evening events are for the whole family.

Interlochen Center for the Arts, PO Box 199, 4000 Highway M-137, Interlochen, MI 49643; (231) 276-7472; fax (231) 276-7464; www.inter-lochen.org/camp. Interlochen Arts Camp is the world's oldest fine arts camp for students age eight to 18. Junior Division campers develop their skills and explore new ones. Talent exploration and development are the main goals of this division, which is unique in that it requires no audition. The waterfront and recreation programs are a very important part of the Junior Division and provide hours of fun and exercise.

National Guitar Workshop, Box 222, Lakeside, CT 06758; (800) 234-6479; (860) 567-3736; www.guitarworkshop.com. Since 1984, the National Guitar Workshop has been dedicated to giving musicians of all ages and skill levels a unique learning experience in a noncompetitive atmosphere with small class sizes, exceptional teachers, and hands-on learning. Students range in age from 13 to 80. Fifty percent of the students are under 18. The camp has programs in many locations in the U.S. Visit the website or write for exact camp locations and dates.

New England Music Camp, PO Box 5200W, 8 Golden Rod Rd., Sidney, ME 04330; (207) 465-3025; www.nemusiccamp.com. NEMC is open to 195 students with a healthy range of musical ability. NEMC rotates orchestra and band seatings weekly. Campers perform a wide variety of music and experience different positions. Campers design individual programs according to their special needs and desires. The weekly program includes two private lessons, participation in one or more major performing groups, and ample practice time. Campers can choose from classes in theory, harmony, composition, conducting, sight singing, jazz appreciation, improvisation, and piano literature.

Power Chord Academy, 7336 Santa Monica Blvd., #107, Los Angeles, CA 90046; (800) 897-6677; fax (775) 306-7923; www.powerchordacademy.com. Young musicians, ages 11 through 17, play in a band, record a CD, make a video, play a concert, and gain an understanding of the music industry.

Strings International Music Festival, 2954 East Grant Ave., Williamstown, NJ 08094; (856) 875-6816; fax (856) 629-6226; www.stringscamp.com. Strings International Music Festival, featuring members of the Philadelphia Orchestra and other internationally acclaimed musicians, is conducted on the grounds of Bryn Mawr College in Bryn Mawr, Pennsylvania. The fourteen-day summer music program is designed for students at every age and skill level—from eight years of age through the college years—and includes four orchestra levels.

Summer Sonatina Piano Camp, 5 Catamount Ln., Bennington, VT 05201; (802) 442-9197; fax (802) 447-3175; www.sonatina.com. Summer Sonatina is an international piano camp for students (ages seven to 16) held in a large historic mansion in Old Bennington, Vermont. Students participate in sight-reading, chorus, theory and composition classes, and many recreational activities.

Usdan Center for the Creative and Performing Arts, www.usdan.com. Long Island office: 185 Colonial Springs Rd., Wheatley Heights, NY 11798; (631) 643-7900. New York office: 420 East 79th St., New York, NY 10021; (212) 772-6060. Usdan Center is a nonprofit summer arts camp, developed in the mid-1960s to become the New York area's "mini-Lincoln Center" on Long Island. Usdan's program offers courses of study in one specific area of its six major departments: music, art, theater, dance, writing, and chess. Students enroll on the basis of interest, except in the piano, jazz ensemble, ballet, theater, jazz and tap, and repertory theater programs, which require auditions.

Young Musicians and Artists, PO Box 13277, Portland, OR 97213; (503) 281-9528; www.ymainc.org. YMA features summer camp programs for children in grades four through 12 in instrumental music, theater, musical theater, choir, piano, dance, technical theater, photography, the visual arts, and creative writing. YMA students increase their artistic skills while building self-esteem and an appreciation for all the performing and visual arts.

Books

Musical Activity and Songbooks

Bonnie Mack Flemming and Darlene Softley Hamilton, *Resources for Creative Teaching in Early Childhood Education*, Harcourt Brace Jovanovich. Extensive resource guide with numerous songs and rhythm activities.

Tom Glazer, *Fifty Musical Finger-Plays*, Doubleday. Songs accompanied by musical scores and suggested dramatizations.

Ella Jenkins, Sherman Krane, and Peggy Lipschultz, *The Ella Jenkins Song Book for Children*, Oak. Ella Jenkins's most requested songs and chants that encourage children to participate and respond.

Francine Klagsbrun, ed., *Free to Be You and Me*, McGraw-Hill. A book of nonsexist, nonracist stories, songs, poems, and drawings. Has a companion album by the same name.

Marian Wirth, Vera Strassevitch, Rita Shotwell, and Patricia Stemmler, *Musical Games, Fingerplays, and Rhythmic Activities for Early Childhood*, Parker.

Building Percussion Instruments

Jay Havighurst, *Making Musical Instruments by Hand*, Rockport.

Bart Hopkin, *Making Simple Musical Instruments: A Melodious Collection of Strings, Winds, Drums, and More*, Lark.

Alex Sabbeth, *Rubber-Band Banjos and a Java Jive Bass: Projects and Activities on the Science of Music and Sound*, John Wiley and Sons.

Mark Shepard, *Simple Flutes: How to Play or Make a Flute of Bamboo, Wood, Clay, Metal, Plastic, or Anything Else*, Shepard.

Jessica Baron Turner and Ronny Susan Schiff, *Let's Make Music! Multicultural Songs and Activities*, Hal Leonard.

Movement and Music

Anne Lief Barlin, *Teaching Your Wings to Fly: The Nonspecialist's Guide to Movement Activities for Young Children*, Goodyear.

Elizabeth B. Carlson and Phyllis Weikart, *Guide to Rhythmically Moving*, High/Scope.

Joanne Landy and Keith Burridge, *Ready to Use Fundamental Motor Skills and Movement Activities for Young Children*, Center for Applied Research in Education.

Phyllis Weikart, *Movement Plus Music: Activities for Children, Ages 3 to 7*, High/Scope.

Phyllis Weikart, *Round the Circle: Key Experiences in Movement for Young Children*, High/Scope.

Sensory Integration Disorders

Carol Kranowitz and Larry B. Silver, *The Out-of-Sync Child: Recognizing and Coping with Sensory Integration Dysfunction*, Perigee. Kranowitz collaborated with leading SI authority Lynn A. Balzer-Martin, Ph.D., OTR, to develop an innovative program that screens children for sensory integration dysfunction. This essential book explains everything a parent needs to know in a friendly format with practical vocabulary. A great tool!

Carol Kranowitz and T. J. Wylie, *The Out-of-Sync Child Has Fun*, Perigee. This companion volume to *The Out-of-Sync Child* helps parents provide enjoyable and productive activities at home for their children with sensory integration dysfunction.

Sharon Heller, *Too Loud, Too Bright, Too Fast, Too Tight: What to Do If You Are Sensory Defensive in an Overstimulating World*, HarperCollins. With skill and elegance, Heller describes what many experience day to day with sensory defensiveness. This book brings the dysfunction to light and gives readers ways to cope with and treat it.

Child Development, Learning Styles, and Disabilities

Teri James Bellis, Ph.D., *When the Brain Can't Hear*, Pocket Books. A thorough and clearly written handbook for parents and professionals working with children who have auditory processing disorders.

Susan Bruckner, *The Whole Musician: A Multi-Sensory Guide to Practice, Performance and Pedagogy*, Effey St. Press. Pianist and instructor Susan Bruckner provides insights and practical strategies for music educators who want to teach and reach "the whole child."

Ronald D. Davis, *The Gift of Dyslexia*, Perigree Psychology Press. A pragmatic, creative book filled with excellent techniques for teaching new learning strategies and information to children with dyslexia.

Gary Fisher, Ph.D. and Rhoda Cummings, Ed.D. *The Survival Guide for Kids with LD*, Free Spirit. Written specifically for school-age children with learning disabilities, this little paperback can help young readers understand themselves and acquire healthy coping strategies for educational and social situations.

Janet Z. Giler, *Socially ADDept: A Manual for Parents of Children with ADHD and/or Learning Disabilities*, C.E.S. This book breaks socially appropriate behaviors into bites parents and their kids with A.D.D. can digest. It also gives teachers and parents excellent techniques for meaningful, productive communication with children who have A.D.D. A useful tool for teachers who wish to keep A.D.D. students engaged and in bounds.

Thom Hartmann, Edward M. Hallowell, and Michael Popkin, *Attention Deficit Disorder: A Different Perception*, Underwood. This book puts A.D.D. in a positive evolutionary context, giving A.D.D. readers a constructive and exciting view of themselves and their lives. Parenting tips and a celebration of A.D.D. ingenuity, energy, and creativity make this book indispensable.

Martin Henley, Roberta S. Ramsey, and Robert Algozzine, *Characteristics of and Strategies for Teaching Students with Mild Disabilities*, Allyn and Bacon. This definitive textbook for teachers presents the range of learning disabilities in a clear, organized fashion. If a child's music teacher wants to develop effective teaching strategies for working with children who have LDs, this tome is a good place to start.

Barbara D. Ingersoll, *Distant Drums, Different Drummers: A Guide for Young People with ADHD*, Cape Publications. This children's book presents kids with an upbeat view of A.D.H.D., honoring their special qualities and giving them a chance to see the so-called disorder in a positive context, placing them historically alongside great explorers and adventurers. A good read when a child receives the A.D.H.D. diagnosis.

Mariaemma Willis and Victoria Kindle-Hodson, *Discover Your Child's Learning Style*, Prima Publishing. This somewhat controversial book provides parents with food for thought and useful tools for understanding exactly how their children learn best. Containing excellent self-assessments and very specific feedback along with detailed descriptions of learning styles and talents, the book puts forth a new model that presses beyond the usual visual, spatial, and auditory styles. For instance, a visual learner may be described as a "print learner" or a "picture learner." It's possible that this model fits some children better than others.

Barbara Strauch, *The Primal Teen*, Doubleday. The author, medical science and health editor at the New York Times, presents a combination of current research on adolescent brain development with parent and teen dialogue and testimony about the ups, downs, and changes of adolescence. It provides valuable new insights into adolescent potential.

Musical Development

Robert Jourdain, *Music, the Brain, and Ecstacy*, Avon.

Dorothy T. McDonald and Gene M. Simons, *Musical Growth and Development: Birth through Six*, Schirmer.

John M. Ortiz, Ph.D., *Nurturing Your Child with Music: How Sound Awareness Creates Happy, Smart, and Confident Children*, Beyond Words.

Sources

The BabyPlus Company, 8906 East 96th St., No. 123, Fishers, IN 46038-9648; (317) 815-1111; (800) 330-6944; fax (317) 815-0041; www.babyplus.com. For the BabyPlus prenatal education system.

Hal Leonard Corp., 7777 W. Bluemound Rd., Milwaukee, WI 53213; (800) 524-4425; www.halleonard.com. For other products by Jessica Baron Turner and an extensive catalog of sheet music, music books, and recordings for children.

Homespun Tapes, PO Box 340, Woodstock, NY 12498; (845) 246-2550; orders (800) 338-2737; fax (845) 246-5282; www.homespuntapes.com. Instructional videos for learning to play musical instruments.

Kimbo Educational, PO Box 477, Long Branch, NJ 07740; (800) 631-2187, fax (732) 870-3340; www.kimboed.com. Catalog of recordings and videos for children, many that make early childhood movement activities fun and easy to conduct.

Lark in the Morning, PO Box 799, Fort Bragg, CA 95437; (707) 964-5569; fax (707) 964-1979; www.larkinthemorning.com. Lark in the Morning sells instruments, music, and more and has shops in Seattle, San Francisco, and Mendocino, California.

Music for Little People, PO Box 1460, Redway, CA 95560-1460; (707) 923-3991; (800) 346-4445; www.musicforlittlepeople.com. Music for Little People is an award-winning producer of music as well as a catalog resource for families searching for the best music and musical products for children.

The Teaching Company, 4151 Lafayette Center Drive, Suite 100, Chantilly, VA 20151-1232; (800) 832-2412; fax (703) 378-3819; www.teach12.com. Audio courses on music such as those taught by professor Robert Greenberg.

Rhythm Fusion Store, 1541-C Pacific Ave., Santa Cruz, CA 95060; (831) 423-2048; (831) 426-7975; fax (831) 423-2073; www.rhythmfusion.com. Percussion of the world: drums, rattles, bells, shakers, and other sound-makers imported from many countries.

Bibliography and References

Andress, B. 1986. Toward an Integrated Developmental Theory for Early Childhood Music. *Bulletin of the Council for Research in Music Education*, 86.

Apfelstadt, H. 1986. Learning Modality: A Potential Clue in the Search for Vocal Accuracy. *Update: The Applications of Research in Music Education*, 4:3.

Arlinger, S., C. Elberling, C. Bak, B. Kofoed, J. Lebech, and K. Saermark. 1982. Cortical Magnetic Fields Evoked by Frequency Glides of a Continuous Tone. *EEG and Clinical Neurophysiology*, 54.

Bachem, A. 1937. Various Types of Absolute Pitch. *Journal of the Acoustical Society of America*, 9.

Bachem, A. 1954. Time Factors in Relative and Absolute Pitch Determination. *Journal of the Acoustical Society of America*, 26.

Baliello, De Poli, and Nobili. 1998. The Colour of Music: Spectral Characterisation of Musical Sounds Filtered by a Cochlear Model. *JNMR*, 4.

Baggaley, J. 1974. Measurement of Absolute Pitch. *Psychology of Music*.

Barnea, A., R. Granot, and H. Pratt. 1994. Absolute Pitch— Electrophysiological Evidence. *International Journal of Psychophysiology*.

Begley, S. 1991. Do You Hear What I Hear? *Newsweek*, Special Issue (Summer).

Begley, S. 1996. Your Child's Brain. *Newsweek* (February 19).

Bellis, T. J. 2002. When the Brain Can't Hear. Pocket Books.

Besson, M., F. Faita, and J. Requin. 1994. Brain Waves Associated with Musical Incongruities Differ for Musicians and Nonmusicians. *Neuroscience Letters*, 168.

Bever, T. G., and R. J. Chiarello. 1974. Cerebral Dominance in Musicians and Nonmusicians. *Science*, 185.

Brady, P. T. 1970. Fixed-Scale Mechanism of Absolute Pitch. *Journal of the Acoustical Society of America*, 48.

Burns, E. M., and S. L. Campbell. 1994. Frequency and Frequency-Ratio Resolution by Possessors of Absolute and Relative Pitch: Examples of Categorical Perception? *Journal of the Acoustical Society of America*, 96.

Chaloupka, V., S. Mitchell, and R. Muirhead. 1994. Observation of a Reversible, Medication-Induced Change in Pitch Perception. *Journal of the Acoustical Society of America*, 96.

Chung, D. Y., and F. B. Colavita. 1976. Periodicity Pitch Perception and Its Upper Frequency Limit in Cats. *Perception and Psychophysics*, 20.

Clarkson, M. G., and R. K. Clifton. 1985. Infant Pitch Perception: Evidence for Responding to Pitch Categories and the Missing Fundamental. *Journal of the Acoustical Society of America*, 77.

Costa-Giomi, E. 1999. The Effects of Three Years of Piano Instruction on Children's Cognitive Development. *Journal of Research in Music Education* (Fall), 47.

Costall, A. 1985. The Relativity of Absolute Pitch. In P. Howell, I. Cross, and R. West, eds., *Musical Structure and Cognition*. London: Academic.

Cousins and Persellin, D. 1999. The Effect of Curwen Hand Signs on Vocal Accuracy of Young Children. *Texas Music Education Research*.

Crummer, G. C., J. P. Walton, J. W. Wayman, E. C. Hantz, and R. D. Frisina. 1994. Neural Processing of Musical Timbre by Musicians, Non-muscians, and Musicians Possessing Absolute Pitch. *Journal of the Acoustical Society of America*, 95.

Cuddy, L. L. 1968. Practice Effects in the Absolute Judgement of Pitch. *Journal of the Acoustical Society of America*.

Cuddy, L. L. 1970. Training the Absolute Identification of Pitch. *Perception and Psychophysics*.

Davidson, L., P. McKernon, and H. Gardner. 1981. The Acquisition of Song: A Developmental Approach. Documentary Report of the Ann Arbor Symposium. Reston, Virginia: Music Educators National Conference.

Davis, M. 1994. Folk Music Psychology. *The Psychologist*, 7.

Deliege, I., and J. Sloboda. 2000. Musical Beginnings: Origins and Development of Musical Competence. New York: Oxford.

Dennis, C. 1975. The Conditioning of a Pitch Response Using Uncertain Singers. In C. K. Madsen, R. D.

Dissanayake, E. 2000. Antecedents of the Temporal Arts in Early Mother-Infant Interaction.

Fagan, Prigot, Carroll, Pioli, Stein, and Franco. 1997. The Role of Music for Infant Memory. *Child Development*, Vol. 68.

Farina, Langhoff, and Tronchin. Acoustic Characterisation of "Virtual" Musical Instruments: Using MLS Technique on Ancient Violins.

Fauna Communications Research Institute. www.animalvoice.com.

Fyk, J. 1995/96. Musical Determinants of Melodic Contour Recognition: Evidence from Experimental Studies of Preschoolers. *Bulletin of the Council for Research in Music Education* (Winter), 127.

Gembris, H. 2002. The Development of Musical Abilities. In R. Colwell and C. Richardson, eds., *The New Handbook of Research on Music Teaching and Learning*, 487–508. New York: Oxford.

Gilbert, J. 1980. An Assessment of Motor Music Skill Development in Young Children. *Journal of Research in Music Education* (Fall), 28(3).

Goetze, M., N. Cooper, and C. Brown. 1990. Recent Research on Singing in the General Music Classroom. *Bulletin of the Council of Research in Music Education* (Spring), 104.

Grandin, Temple, Peterson, Matthew, Shaw, L. Gordon. 1998. Spatial-Temporal Versus Language-Analytic Reasoning: The Role of Music Training. Musical training improves a child's ability in spatial-temporal reasoning, which is important in mathematics and science education. *Arts Education Policy Review* (July/August).

Green, G. 1990. The Effect of Vocal Modeling on Pitch-Matching Accuracy of Elementary School Children. *Journal of Research in Music Education*, 38:3.

Greer and C. H. Madsen, Jr., eds. Research in Music Behavior: Modifying Music Behavior in the Classroom. New York: Teachers College Press.

Greer, D., L. Dorrow, and A. Randall. 1974. Music Listening Preferences of Elementary School Children. *Journal of Research in Music Education*, 22.

Groves, W. C. 1969. Rhythmic Training and Its Relationship to the Synchronization of Motor-Rhythmic Responses. *Journal of Research in Music Education* (Winter), 7(4).

Halpern, A. R. 1989. Memory for the Absolute Pitch of Familiar Songs. *Memory and Cognition*, 17.

Hedden, S. 1980. Development of Music Listening Skills. *Bulletin of the Council for Research in Music Education*, 64.

Hendley, J., and D. Persellin. 1996. The Comparative Effects of the Lower Adult Male Voice and the Male Falsetto Voice on Children's Vocal Accuracy. *Update: Applications of Research in Music Education*, 14:2.

Hetland, L. 2000. Learning to Make Music Enhances Spatial Reasoning. In E. Winner and L. Hetland, eds., *Journal of Aesthetic Education*, 34.

Hodges, Donald A. 2002. Musicality from Birth to Five. Institute for Music Research, MUSICA, *IFMR News* (Summer), Vol. 1, No. 1.

Hulse, S. H., J. Cynx, and J. Humpal. 1984. Absolute and Relative Pitch Discrimination in Serial Pitch Perception by Birds. *Journal of Experimental Psychology*: General.

Imberty, M. 1996. Linguistic and Musical Development in Preschool and School-Age Children. In I. Deliege and J. Sloboda, eds., *Musical beginnings: Origins and Development of Musical Competence*. New York: Oxford.

Jeffress, L. A. 1962. Absolute Pitch. *Journal of the Acoustical Society of America*, 34.

Jourdain, R. 1998. Music, the Brain, and Ecstacy. Avon Books.

Lamont, A. 1998. The Development of Cognitive Representations of Musical Pitch. Unpublished doctoral dissertation, University of Cambridge.

LeBlanc, A., and R. Cote. 1983. Effects of Tempo and Performing Medium on Children's Music Preference. *Journal of Research in Music Education*, 31:1.

Lecanuet, J. 1996. Prenatal Auditory Experience. In I. Deliege and J. Sloboda, eds., *Musical Beginnings: Origins and Development of Musical Competence.* New York: Oxford.

Levitin, D. J. 1994. Absolute Memory for Musical Pitch: Evidence from the Production of Learned Melodies. *Perception and Psychophysics.*

Lockhead, G. R., and R. Byrd. 1981. Practically Perfect Pitch. *Journal of the Acoustical Society of America.*

McDonald, D., and G. Simons. 1989. Musical Growth and Development: Birth through Six. New York: Schirmer Books.

McDonald, D. T., and J. H. Ramsey, 1979. A Study of Musical Auditory Information Processing of Preschool Children. *Contributions to Music Education.*

Meyer, M. 1899. Is the Memory of Absolute Pitch Capable of Development by Training? *Psychological Review, 6.*

Miyazaki, K. 1992. Perception of Musical Intervals by Absolute Pitch Possessors. *Music Perception, 9.*

Moog, H. 1976. The Development of Musical Experience in Children of Pre-school Age. *Psychology of Music,* 4(2).

Moore, B. C. J. 1997. An Introduction to the Psychology of Hearing (fourth edition). San Diego and London: Academic Press.

Murphy C., and D. Persellin. 1993. Improving Vocal Accuracy of First Graders through Learning Modalities. *Texas Music Education Research.*

Ortiz, John M., Ph.D., 1999. Nurturing your Child with Music: How Sound Awareness Creates Happy, Smart, and Confident Children. Beyond Words Publishing.

Pantev, C., R. Oostenveld, A. Engelien, B. Ross, L. E. Roberts, and M. Hoek. 1998. Increased Auditory Cortical Representation. *Nature.*

Papousek, M. 1996. Intuitive Parenting: A Hidden Source of Musical Stimulation in Infancy. In I. Deliege and J. Sloboda, eds., *Musical Beginnings: Origins and Development of Musical Competence,* 88–112. New York: Oxford.

Persellin, D. 1993. The Effect of Learning Modalities when Used in Pitch Matching of Patterns within Complete Songs. *Perceptual and Motor Skills,* 76:1.

Persellin, D. 2002. Research on Music Teaching and Learning During Elementary School Years. *Trinity University IFMR News* (Summer), Vol. 1, No. 1.

Pflederer, M. 1964, Winter. The Responses of Children to Musical Tasks Embodying Piaget's Principle of Conservation. *Journal of Research in Music Education*, 12(4).

Pouthas, V. 1996. The Development of the Perception of Time and Temporal Regulation of Action in Infants and Children. In I. Deliege and J. Sloboda, eds., *Musical Beginnings: Origins and Development of Musical Competence*, 115–141. New York: Oxford.

Profita, J., and T. G. Bidder. 1988. Perfect Pitch. *American Journal of Medical Genetics*, 29.

Rainbow, E. 1981. A Final Report on a Three-Year Investigation of the Rhythmic Abilities of Pre-School Aged Children. *Bulletin of the Council for Research in Music Education*.

Rakowski, A., and M. Morawska-Büngeler. 1987. In Search of the Criteria for Absolute Pitch. *Archives of Acoustics*.

Ramsey, J. H. 1983. The Effects of Age, Singing Ability, and Instrumental Experiences on Preschool Children's Melodic Perception. *Journal of Research in Music Education*, 31(2).

R. Parncutt and G. McPherson. 2002. *The Science and Psychology of Music Performance*. New York: Oxford.

Rutkowski, J. 1996. The Effectiveness of Individual/Small-group Singing Activities on Kindergartner's Use of Singing Voice and Developmental Music Aptitude. *Journal of Research in Music Education*, 44 :4.

Sacks, O. 1995. Musical Ability. *Science*.

Schlaug, G., L. Jäncke, Y. Huang, and H. Steinmetz. 1995. In Vivo Evidence of Structural Brain Asymmetry in Musicians. *Science*.

Scott, C. R. 1979. Pitch Concept Formation in Pre-School Children. *Bulletin of the Council for Research in Music Education*.

Sergent, D. 1969. Experimental Investigation of Absolute Pitch. *Journal of Research in Music Education*, 17.

Shatz, C. 1992. The Developing Brain. *Scientific American*, 267:3.

Simons, G. 1986. Early Childhood Musical Development: A Survey of Selected Research. *Bulletin of the Council for Research in Music Education*, 86.

Sims, W. 1987. Effects of Tempo on Music Preference of Pre-School Through Fourth-Grade Children. In C. Madsen and C. Prickett, eds., *Applications of Research in Music Behavior*, 15–25. Tuscaloosa: University of Alabama.

Stevens, S. S. 1935. The Relation of Pitch to Intensity. *Journal of the Acoustical Society of America*, 6.

Terhardt, E., and M. Seewann. 1983. Aural Key Identication and Its Relationship to Absolute Pitch. *Music Perception*, 1.

Trehub, S., D. Bull, and L. Thorpe. 1984. Infants' Perceptions of Melodies: The Role of Melodic Contour. *Child Development*, 55.

Vispoel, W. P. and J. R. Austin. 1993. Constructive Response to Failure in Music: The Role of Attribution Feedback and Classroom Goal Structure. *British Journal of Educational Psychology*, 63:110–129.

Wallin, N., B. Merker, and S. Brown, eds. *The Origins of Music*. Cambridge, Mass.: MIT Press.

Ward, W. D. 1999. Absolute Pitch. In D. Deutsch, ed., *The Psychology of Music*. San Diego: Academic Press.

Webster, P. R., and K. Schlentrich. 1982. Discrimination of Pitch Direction by Preschool Children with Verbal and Nonverbal Tasks. *Journal of Research in Music Education*, 30(3).

Weinberger, N. M. 2001 Musical Talent: Real or a Myth? *MuSICA Research Notes*, Vol. VIII, Issue 2 (Summer).

Welch, G. 1985. Variability of Practice and Knowledge of Results as Factors in Learning to Sing in Tune. *Bulletin of the Council for Research in Music Education*, 85.

Whitfield, I. C. 1980. Auditory Cortex and the Pitch of Complex Tones. *Journal of the Acoustical Society of America*, 67(2).

Winnicott, D. W. 1971. Playing and Reality. Routledge.

Williamson, S., and L. Kaufman. 1988. Auditory Evoked Magnetic Fields. In A. Jahn and J. Santos-Sacchi, eds., *Physiology of the Ear*, 497–505. New York: Raven Press.

Yarbrough, C., G. Green, W. Benson, and J. Bowers. 1991. Inaccurate Singers: An Exploratory Study of Variables Affecting Pitch-Matching. *Bulletin for the Council for Research in Music Education* (Winter).

Youngson, S., and D. Persellin. 2001. The Effect of Curwen Hand Signs on Vocal Accuracy of Young Children. *Kodály Envoy*, 27:2.

Zatorre, R. J. 1988. Pitch Perception of Complex Tones and Human Temporal-lobe Function. *Journal of the Acoustical Society of America*.

Zatorre, R. J., and C. Beckett. 1989. Multiple Coding Strategies in the Retention of Musical Tones by Possessors of Absolute Pitch. *Memory and Cognition*.

About the Author

Jessica Baron Turner is an award-winning author, music educator, and child development specialist, and, above all else, she is a mother. Her *SmartStart Guitar* method books and recordings have become America's best-selling approach to guitar education for young children. Her readers and students benefit from Ms. Turner's inclusive style and supportive, humorous tone. She believes all of us are musical by nature and feels privileged to help students of every age discover and develop their musical talents and creativity. Her recently co-authored publication *Guitarra de SmartStart, metódo y cancionero* presents 26 vibrant songs from Spanish-speaking countries with lyrics in both Spanish and English, alongside the *SmartStart Guitar* method translated for the first time.

Ms. Turner holds a bachelor of arts degree in child development and a master's degree in clinical psychology, and is currently pursuing postgraduate training in special education. She teaches general and vocal music in elementary schools and has been teaching guitar and voice lessons privately for 25 years.

Ms. Turner founded and directs Guitars in the Classroom, a non-profit program operating under the auspices of the San Francisco Community Initiative Funds. Guitars in the Classroom provides free guitar and music facilitation training to interested elementary school classroom teachers so that making music can become an exciting part of any elementary classroom. She lives in Santa Cruz, California, with her husband, luthier Rick Turner; their son, Elias; plus 25 fish, two frogs, two cats, and two blue-bellied western fence lizards.

About the Photographer

Gayle Mitchell's life has been blessed with two wonderful boys, close family ties, and a career in both maternal child nursing and portrait photography. She is passionate about capturing moments which embrace the heart of the human spirit. From birth to the end of life, Gayle feels fortunate to connect with others in times of joy and aid in their moments of sadness.

"The children in the photos gave their heart to their music and I enjoyed watching their smiles grow as their music played" she recalls. "Their creativity and pleasure was a joy to observe."

Gayle lives, works, and plays in Santa Cruz, California where the ocean and redwoods fill her with appreciation for all the beauty life offers.

Testimonials

"In a time when children are bottom-line over-tested, over-assessed, and over-scheduled, Jessica Baron Turner provides an inspiring and practical musical antidote in *Your Musical Child*. She guides parents to help discover the magic of musical experience their children—a powerful, joyful way they can provide the full impact of music as a creative joy and not just another activity. Ms. Turner has the priorities just right, as other books miss—emphasizing the natural fun, personal curious exploration that music can and should provide. Follow the excellent suggestions in *Your Musical Child*, and the beginning musician in your home will not only gain all the cognitive, social, and creative benefits music can provide, but will also have great fun all along the way. Begin a lifetime relationship with music just right—follow the inspiring path laid out so beautifully in *Your Musical Child*. It makes me wish I were six and just beginning the violin, with my mom holding Jessica Baron Turner's book in her hands."

– Eric Booth,
Education Faculty of Juilliard, Tanglewood and
The Kennedy Center National Arts in Education leader

"I read *Your Musical Child* with great interest because it poses and answers many questions parents have about their role in the music education of their children. In addition to Jessica Baron Turner's "braid" analogy, a similar three faceted "braid" analogy could be made between the student, the parents, and the music teacher, each having a distinct role and responsibilities. MENC: the National Association for Music Education applauds Ms. Turner's desire, effort, and thoroughness in providing parents with the information, resources, and encouragement to meet their responsibilities and to play an active role in this important part of their child's development and music education."

– David Circle
President Elect of Music Educators National Conference, MENC

"As a consulting clinician I am always trying to find ways to help parents be partners in their children's development. Jessica Baron Turner's new book, *Your Musical Child*, presents a unique, developmental, and practical approach to helping parents nurture their children's growing musicality—one that educators and family therapists are also sure to find informative and encouraging. Her clear explanations of learning styles, combined with strategic suggestions for musical activities tailored to children's specific ages and stages may be any parent's indispensable tool for making decisions at those crucial moments when it's important to understand what one's child truly needs. This book is well-organized and exceptionally informative, its reach extending beyond the realm of music into the heart of what good parenting is all about."

– Marina L. Eovaldi, Ph.D.
Licensed Clinical Psychologist and Family Therapist
Northwestern University Family Institute

"As you read these words of mine, I realize that I wouldn't be talking to you right now if it hadn't been for the encouragement and support that my mother and father gave me when, at the age of 13, I chose a life of music. When other friends' parents were begging their kids to get "a real job," all my parents wanted me to do was to follow my heart.

I believe that the first prerequisite for being a musician is having PASSION for music. I was passionate and my parents were right there for me. The rest is history.

Please encourage your children to express themselves joyfully through music and to use music to communicate with others. What a way to find a little peace. This book will help you find a new relationship with your child, and perhaps, yourself. It's never too late."

– Graham Nash
Singer, Songwriter, Recording and Performing Artist
Los Angeles, California

"*Your Musical Child: Inspiring Kids to Play and Sing for Keeps* by music educator Jessica Baron Turner is a guidebook to nurturing musical talent in children. Practical advice concerning everything from in utero exposure to music to selecting an instrument that is right for one's child; to encouraging regular practicing without overdoing it; to selecting properly qualified teachers and so much more make *Your Musical Child* very strongly recommended reading for any parents or caregiver with a musically inclined child in their charge."

– Midwest Book Review,
March, 2004

OTHER GREAT PUBLICATIONS
BY JESSICA BARON TURNER

LET'S MAKE MUSIC!
AN INTERACTIVE
MUSICAL TRIP
AROUND THE WORLD
by Jessica Baron Turner
This unique book/audio
package lets children sing and
play songs from around the
world by making their own
musical instruments. The book
includes easy-to-follow instructions for making and
playing 10 percussion instruments by using recycled,
everyday items. Each instrument project includes background information on its culture of origin, activities and
games involving the instrument, a suggested reading list
for more information on the culture, and a song to play
with the instrument.
00815057 Book/CD Pack $19.95

LET'S MAKE MUSIC
*by Jessica Baron Turner
and Ronny Schiff*
Bring the diversity of our world
to every classroom through
music with this collection of 11
songs and activities for Grades
K-3. The book introduces 10
multicultural musical instruments and songs from around
the world and includes step-by-step instructions for
making each instrument from recycled and common
household materials. Activities, games, stories and
teaching notes complement each song.
08740178 Song/Activity Book...................................$14.95
08740180 Performance/Accompaniment CD.............$16.95

SMARTSTART GUITAR
A FUN, EASY
APPROACH TO
BEGINNING GUITAR FOR KIDS
by Jessica Baron Turner
This innovative instructional
method is designed for use in
the general music classroom,
and is developmentally structured to get all beginning guitar
students playing and singing from the very first lesson, no
matter what their level of experience. It's easy to use and
before you know it, you'll be helping even young children
to play well and build general music skills, one success at
a time! For ages 5-10.
00695156 Book/CD Pack $12.95
00641365 VHS Video..$19.95
00695281 Value Pack – Book/CD + Video...............$14.47

SMARTSTART GUITAR SONGBOOK
by Jessica Baron Turner
This excellent guitar songbook/CD pack features 43
special songs for home
and school, in arrangements
designed to help beginners of
all ages begin to hear, feel and
remember the music. Songs
include: America • Apples and Bananas • The Boll Weevil
• Casey Jones • The Ballad of John Henry • Lincoln and
Liberty • Shenandoah • Simple Gifts • and more.
00695254 Book/CD Pack $12.95

SMARTSTART GUITAR
AGES 12 & UP
FOR LATE BLOOMERS,
BABY BOOMERS AND THEIR TEENS
by Jessica Baron Turner
This is the ultimate user-friendly
guitar method and songbook
for older kids and adults who
have always wanted to play
guitar! The book contains 17
classic and timeless songs – complete with lyrics – plus
pictures, diagrams, and easy-to-follow song charts to
make learning easy. The accompanying CD features voice
and guitar. Songs include: Amazing Grace • The Cuckoo
• Froggy Went A-Courtin' • House of the Rising Sun • Red
River Valley • and more!
00695364 Book/CD Pack $12.95

GUITARRA DE SMARTSTART (SMARTSTART GUITAR) METHOD AND SONGBOOK (SPANISH/ENGLISH)
*by Jessica Baron Turner,
Alexander Marshall, Cecilia
Phillips & Francisco Rangel*
This book/CD pack teaches guitarists to play and sing 26
beautiful songs in both Spanish and English using classic
tunes such as: Caballito Blanco • Cielito Lindo • De
Colores • Guantanamera • La Cucaracha • La Bamba •
Las Mañanitas • Mi Gallo • and more. It's perfect for
beginning or intermediate level guitar students, Spanish
speakers, English language learners, Latin music fans,
classroom teachers, early childhood educators, and
family sing-alongs! This is the guitar method bilingual
educators have been waiting for!
00695545 Book/CD Pack $16.95